Principles of the Christian Life

A Core Course of the School of Leadership

Church of the Nazarene

Mesoamerica Region

Monica Mastronardi

SCHOOL
OF
LEADERSHIP

Principles of the Christian Life

A book in the "School of Leadership" series.
Core Level Course

Author: Monica Mastronardi de Fernandez
Co-Author: Karla Córdoba

Spanish Editor: Dr. Monica E. Mastronardi de Fernandez
Translators: Dorothy Bullon
Reviewer: Shelley Webb

Material produced by EDUCATION AND CLERGY DEVELOPMENT
of the Church of the Nazarene, Mesoamerica Region. www.edunaz.org
Mailing Address: PO Box 3977 - 1000 San José, Costa Rica, Central América.
Phone (506) 2285-0432 / 0423 - Email: EL@mesoamericaregion.org

Publisher and Distributor: Asociación Región Mesoamérica
Av. 12 de Octubre Plaza Victoria Locales 5 y 6
Pueblo Nuevo Hato Pintado, Ciudad de Panamá
Tel. (507) 203-3541
E-mail: literatura@mesoamericaregion.org

All Biblical quotations are from the New International Version-2011, unless otherwise noted.

Design: Juan Manuel Fernandez (www.juanfernandez.ga)
Cover image by Joshua Jordan
Cover images and interiors of the covers used with permission under license "Bienes Comunes" (Creative Commons).

Digital printing

Table of Contents

Introduction

The book series **School of Leadership** is designed with the purpose of providing a tool to the church for formation, education and training of its members to actively integrate into Christian service the gifts and calling (vocation) they have received from the Lord.

Each book provides study materials for one course in the **School of Leadership** program offered by the theological Institutions of the Mesoamerica Region of the Church of the Nazarene. These institutions include: IBN (Coban, Guatemala); STN (Guatemala City); SENAMEX (Mexico City); SENDAS (San Jose, Costa Rica); SND (Santo Domingo, Dominican Republic); and SETENAC (Havana, Cuba). A number of leaders from these schools (presidents, directors, vice presidents and directors of decentralized academic studies) actively participated in the program design.

The **School of Leadership** has five core courses that are common to all ministries, and six specialized courses for each ministry area, at the end of which, the respective theological institution awards the student a certificate (or diploma) in Specialized Ministry.

The overall objective of the **School of Leadership** is "to work with the local church in equipping the saints for the work of the ministry establishing a solid biblical and theological foundation and developing them through the practice of exercising their gifts for service in the local congregation and society as a whole." The specific objectives of this program are threefold:

- Develop the ministerial gifts of the local congregation.
- Multiply service ministries in the church and community.
- Raise awareness of the vocation of professional ministry in its diverse forms.

We thank Dr. Monica Mastronardi de Fernandez for her dedication as General Editor of the project, and the Regional Coordinators of Ministries and the team of writers and designers who collaborated to publish these books. We are equally grateful to the teachers who will share these materials. They will make a difference in the lives of thousands of people in the Mesoamerica Region and beyond.

Finally, we thank Dr. L. Carlos Saenz, Mesoamerica Regional Director, for his continued support in this work, which is the result of his conviction that the church must be holistically equipped.

We pray for God's blessing for all the disciples whose lives and Christian service will be enriched by these books.

Dr. Ruben E. Fernandez
Theological Education Coordinator
Mesoamerica Region

What Is the School of Leadership?

The School of Leadership is an educational program for lay ministry in different specialties to engage in the mission of the local church. This program is administered by the Theological Institutions of the Church of the Nazarene in the Mesoamerica Region and taught both at these institutions and in the local churches enrolled in the program.

Who Can Benefit from the School of Leadership?

It is for all the members of the Church of the Nazarene who have participated in Levels B and C of the discipleship program, and who, with all their heart, wish to discover their gifts and serve God in His work.

The Plan ABCDE

In order to contribute to the formation of the members of their churches, the Church of the Nazarene in the Mesoamerica Region has adopted the plan of discipleship ABCDE, and since 2001 began publishing materials for each of these levels. The School of Leadership is Level D of the ABCDE discipleship plan and is designed for those who have been through previous levels of discipleship.

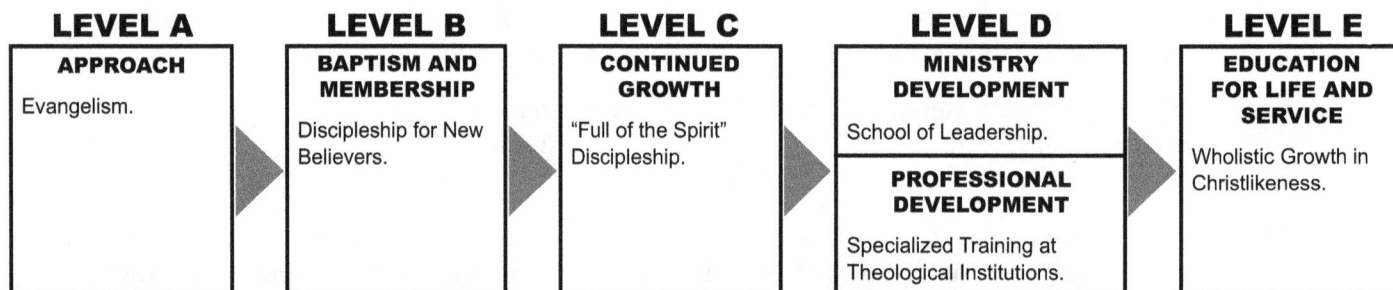

LEVEL A	LEVEL B	LEVEL C	LEVEL D	LEVEL E
APPROACH	**BAPTISM AND MEMBERSHIP**	**CONTINUED GROWTH**	**MINISTRY DEVELOPMENT**	**EDUCATION FOR LIFE AND SERVICE**
Evangelism.	Discipleship for New Believers.	"Full of the Spirit" Discipleship.	School of Leadership.	Wholistic Growth in Christlikeness.
			PROFESSIONAL DEVELOPMENT	
			Specialized Training at Theological Institutions.	

In the Church of the Nazarene, we believe making disciples in the image of Christ in the nations is the foundation of missionary work and the responsibility of leadership (Ephesians 4: 7-16). The work of discipleship is continuous and dynamic; therefore, the disciple never stops growing in the likeness of his Lord. This growth, when healthy, occurs in all dimensions: the individual dimension (spiritual growth), the corporate dimension (joining the congregation), the holiness in life dimension (progressive transformation of our being and doing according to the model of Jesus Christ) and the service dimension (investing our lives in ministry).

Dr. Monica Mastronardi de Fernandez
Managing Editor, The School of Leadership Book Series

How Do I Use This Book?

This book contains eight lessons of the School of Leadership program, along with activities and final evaluation of the course.

How are the contents of this book organized?

Each of the eight lessons of this book contains the following:

➤ **Objectives:** These are the learning objectives the student is expected to understand at the end of the lesson.

➤ **Main Ideas:** A summary of the key teachings of the lesson.

➤ **Development of Lesson:** This is the largest section because it is the development of the contents of the lesson. The lessons have been written so that the book can be the teacher, and for that reason the contents have been written in a dynamic form and in simple language with contemporary ideas.

➤ **Notes and Comments:** The information in the margins is intended to clarify terms and provide notes that complement or extend the content of the lesson.

➤ **Questions:** Sometimes questions are included in the margin that the teacher can use to introduce or reinforce a lesson topic.

➤ **What did we learn?:** The box at the end of the lesson development section provides a brief summary of the lesson.

➤ **Activities:** This is a page at the end of each lesson that contains learning activities, for individuals or groups, on the subject studied. The estimated time for implementation in class is 20 minutes.

➤ **Final evaluation of the course:** This is the last page of the book and once completed the student must remove it from the book and hand it in to a course instructor. The final evaluation should take about 15 minutes.

How long is each course?

The courses are designed for 12 hours of class over 8 ninety-minute sessions. Each institution and each church or local theological study center will coordinate days and times of the classes. Within this hour and a half the teacher or the teachers should include time for the activities contained in the book.

What is the role of the student?

The student is responsible for the following:

1. Enroll on time for the course.
2. Buy the book and study each lesson before class time.
3. Arrive for class on time.
4. Participate in class activities.
5. Participate in practical ministry in the local church outside of class.
6. Complete and submit the final evaluation to the teacher.

What is the role of the teacher of the course?

The professors and teachers for the School of Leadership courses are pastors and laity committed to the mission and ministry of the church and preferably have experience in the ministry they teach. The Director and/or the School of Leadership at the local church (or theological institution) invites their participation and their functions are the following:

1. Be well prepared by studying the book's content and scheduling the use of class time. When studying the lesson, you should have on hand the Bible and a dictionary. Although the lessons are written using simple language, it is recommended that you "translate" what you consider difficult in order to help the students understand. In other words, use terms that they can better understand.

2. Ensure that the students are studying the material in the book and achieving the learning objectives.

3. Plan and accompany students in the activities of ministerial practice. The local pastor and the director of the respective ministry must schedule these activities. These activities should not take away from class time.

4. Take daily attendance and grades in the class report form. The final average will be the result demonstrated by the student in the following activities:

   a. Class work
   b. Participation in ministerial practice outside of class
   c. Final evaluation

5. At the end of the course, collect the evaluation sheets and hand them in with the form "Class Report" to the local School of Leadership director. Do this after totaling the averages and verifying that all data is complete on the form.

6. Professors and teachers should not add tasks or reading assignments apart from the contents of the book. They should be creative in the design of the learning activities and in planning ministry activities outside the classroom according to the reality of their local church and its context.

How do I teach a class?

We recommend using a 90-minute class session as follows:

• **5 minutes:** Review the topic of the previous lesson and pray together.

• **30 minutes:** Review and discuss the lesson. We recommend using an outline, chalkboard, cardboard or other available materials, using dynamic learning activities and visual media such as graphics, drawings, objects, pictures, questions, assigning students to submit parts of the lesson, and so on. We do not recommend lecturing or having the teacher reread the lesson content.

• **5 minutes:** Break either in the middle of class or when it is convenient.

• **20 minutes:** Work on activities in the book. This can be done at the beginning, middle or end of the review, or you can complete the activities as you proceed in accordance with the issues as it relates to them.

• **20 minutes:** Discussion about the students' ministry practice that they currently do and that they will do. At the beginning of the course you will need to present the schedule to the students so that they can make arrangements to attend the ministry practice. In the classes when the students discuss their ministry practice, the conversation should be focused on what they learned, including their successes and their errors, as well as the difficulties they encountered.

• **10 minutes:** Prayer for the issues arising from the practice (challenges, people, problems, goals, gratitude for the results, among others).

How do I implement the final course evaluation?

Allocate 15 minutes of time during the last class meeting for the course evaluation. If necessary, students may consult their books and Bibles. Final evaluations are designed to be an activity to reinforce what was learned in class and not a repetition of the contents of the book. The purpose of this assessment is to measure the understanding and evaluation of the student concerning the class topics, their spiritual growth, their progress in the commitment to the mission of the church and their progress in ministerial experience.

Ministerial Practice Activities

The following are suggested activities for ministerial practice outside of class. The list below includes several ideas to help teachers, pastors, directors of local School of Leadership groups and local ministry directors. From the list you can choose the activity best suited to the contextual situation and the local church ministry, or replace these with others according to the needs and possibilities of your context.

We recommend having at least three ministerial activities per course. You can put the whole class to work on a project or assign group tasks according to interests, gifts and abilities. It is advisable to involve students in a variety of new ministry experiences.

Suggested Ministry Activities for Principles of the Christian Life

1. During the time of this course, each student disciples a new believer using the *New Life in Christ* lessons (Level B, Discipleship Plan A,B,C,D,E).

2. A student group designs a plan to reaffirm the Articles of Faith of the Church of the Nazarene. This plan should be implemented during a worship service(s) in a creative manner using the abilities of the group members.

3. Design an invitation for an evangelistic event on the topic of "Who is Jesus?" The event could be a breakfast, an afternoon tea or coffee meeting, a dinner or another activity. (This could be combined with numbers 4 and 5 below).

4. Invite family members, friends and neighbors to an evangelistic activity using the invitations from #3 above. To make it interesting, begin the time by having people mention a question they have about Jesus. Take note of these questions so you can use them later as a guide for the development of activities.

5. Design an evangelistic activity using music or talent show combined with an evangelistic message on the topic of "Who is Jesus?" (This activity can be combined with #3 and #4 above).

6. Organize a drawing class for children on the topic of "What is the purpose of the church?"

7. In the first week of the course, survey the congregation to identify who has not had the experience of being filled with the Holy Spirit. Later, during the month of the course, you can pray for these people that they will be filled with God's power.

8. Organize a time of spiritual retreat for one day or for one weekend for the purpose of praying and learning about how to be filled with the Holy Spirit. This could be for a small group or for the entire congregation. (This activity could be combined with #7).

WHO IS GOD?

- To identify erroneous teachings about God.
- To understand what the Bible teaches about God.
- To appreciate the God of holy love.

- God exists and He has revealed Himself in three distinct persons: Father, Son and Holy Spirit.
- Theology helps us study the amazing qualities of our God.
- The two outstanding qualities of the character of God are holiness and love.

Introduction

The purpose of this lesson is to understand the fundamental truths that the Bible teaches about God. We begin by clarifying that no human being, with his or her limited intellect, can completely understand the magnificent Creator of the universe. However, the Bible provides instruction for us so that we can better understand our God, and therefore be able to approach and relate to Him. With the help of theology, we will study the topic: "Who is God?"

What is the image of God in your community?

What is theology? Theology is the orderly study of the truth about God and His relationship with people as revealed to us in the Scriptures. Theology is the science that helps us to answer the most important questions about life: Where did I come from? What is my purpose in life? Where will I go when I die? Theology is as necessary to the Christian faith as the skeleton is for the human body. The Christian needs to know and understand the truths that are declared in the Bible so that he or she can teach them, live them and defend them.

Is the Christian God One Among Other "gods?"

People have created many false "gods."

"Now this is eternal life: that they know you, the only true God, and Jesus Christ, whom you have sent" (John 17:3 NIV).

In the Old Testament, anything or anyone that was an object of worship, other than God, was considered to be an "idol" that is, something that was usurping the place that only belongs to God. The Old Testament prophets constantly denounced the folly of those who trusted in "gods" made by human hands, created by human beings according to their needs and selfish whims.

According to Professor Orton Wiley, idolatry is "to give divine status to idols, images, or any object, including excessive admiration, devotion or love for a person or thing."

Some "Christian" groups have spread the concept of a "god" who is at the service of mankind. This "god" is one who can be manipulated to indulge the wishes of his "servants." Others, who follow "prosperity theology," conceive of God as one whose priority is to provide "economic prosperity" for those who worship and serve Him. Another group turns to God to help them only in times of need, like the windshield wipers of our cars, which we use only when it rains.

Why do people prefer a "god" of their own making instead of getting to know the one true God? Because human beings are very comfortable being their own "gods" and living their lives as if God does not exist. The problem is that if they were to recognize that there is a God who is creator and owner of everything, then they must also accept that this God has a right to be the Lord and Master of their lives and acknowledging this would lead them to change their lifestyle, no longer living a life guided by the whims of self-will.

"I, even I, am the Lord, and apart from me there is no savior" (Isaiah 43:11).

In summary, those who deny the existence of God or are not interested in knowing the true God, are not willing to take responsibility before the Supreme Being (Romans 1:28-29). For a person to reach the point of acknowledging God as Lord of their life, several obstacles must be crossed:

- The first hurdle is to admit that God exists, which is difficult because people do not want to lose the freedom to live according to their desires and pleasures.

- The second obstacle is to recognize that God is the sovereign Creator of all things (including human beings). This is difficult because it involves accepting that God is in control of life and committing to being accountable to Him for how life is lived.

- The third is to give God what He alone deserves: worship. This involves moving the center of worship from oneself to God, but this is difficult because people always want to be recognized and receive the glory.

In Christian literature and in the Bible when the word "God" is written with a capital "G" it refers to the one true God, but when the word "god" is written with a small "g" it refers to false gods, even if the people who worship them believe in them.

People are wrong to think they have the right to judge, to receive glory, and to exercise authority or power over their own lives and the lives of others. To usurp the place of God or claim the right that belongs to the Lord God is the same temptation that Satan presented to Adam and Eve when he provoked in them the desire to "be like God" (Genesis 3:4-5).

"For I Am God and There Is No Other"

The Bible reveals the one true God.

The prophet Isaiah proclaimed that Jehovah is the only true God, the Almighty, maker of heaven and earth, Lord of lords and King of kings. Isaiah 45: 21-22 says: *"Declare what is to be, present it—let them take counsel together. Who foretold this long ago, who declared it from the distant past? Was it not I, the LORD? And there is no God apart from me, a righteous God and a Savior; there is none but me. Turn to me and be saved, all you ends of the earth; for I am God, and there is no other."* The prophet made this statement when all of Israel's neighbors were polytheistic, which means they worshiped many different gods. Unfortunately, Israel also fell into that same sin.

To study the nature of God, refer to these Scriptures:
Isaiah 6:1-7, 45:20-23
Exodus 3:14-15
Deuteronomy 33:27
Psalm 16:2; 102: 27
Isaiah 45:20-21
1 John 4:7-1
1 Timothy 1: 17
Revelation 4:8

Isaiah teaches that God is totally different from the "gods" created by man. For the people of that time, it was difficult to accept the idea of a creator God, almighty, unique and sustainer of all that exists. For this reason, they had many gods that were represented by images in the likeness of human beings or animals. These gods had the same human weaknesses and imperfections, but their worshipers believed they were "bigger" and "more powerful" than themselves. No doubt they wanted to represent in those "idols" their desire to "be like gods," the desire that Satan, in the form of a serpent, placed in the human heart in the Garden of Eden (Genesis 3:4-5).

Are Christians Polytheists Because We Believe in a Triune God?

Do Christians have one God or three Gods?

The teachings of Jesus in the Gospel of John chapters 14 and 16 are helpful to understand the mystery of the Trinity. The Master taught that there is the Father, the Son and the Holy Spirit, who exist and interact in perfect communion, in unity and love, and that these three are one and the same God. Men and women cannot go to the Father (Philippians 4:20) without interacting first with the Son (Matthew 1:21, Titus 1:3), and they cannot relate to the Son without relying on the Holy Spirit (Ephesians 2:18).

No doubt this truth revealed in Scripture goes beyond what our reason can take in, but that does not mean it is not true. It is a reality that can only be accepted by faith.

The Father, the Son and the Holy Spirit work together in the mission of rescuing human beings from their sin. They continually work to bring salvation to all the families of the earth, but they never do this independently, but as a team and by directing the ministry of the Church.

Who Is God?

God has unique qualities that distinguish Him from all other living beings.

When trying to describe God, we must talk about His nature, that is, those attributes (characteristics or qualities) that only He possesses. Theology organizes and describes these characteristics, which are summarized in the following table:

"We believe in one eternally existent, infinite God, Sovereign Creator and Sustainer of the universe; that He only is God, holy in nature, attributes, and purpose. The God who is holy love and light is Triune in essential being, revealed as Father, Son, and Holy Spirit." (Genesis 1; Leviticus 19:2; Deuteronomy 6:4-5; Isaiah 5:16; 6:1-7; 40:18-31; Matthew 3:16-17; 28:19-20; John 14:6-27; 1 Corinthians 8:6; 2 Corinthians 13:14; Galatians 4:4-6; Ephesians 2:13-18; 1 John 1:5; 4:8)" (Article of Faith No. 1, Manual of the Church of the Nazarene 2009-2013, pg. 28).

Attributes of God	Description	Passages
Eternal	The existence of God has no beginning or end. He is the beginning and the end. God existed before history began and will exist after it.	Job 36: 26; Psalm 90:2, 102:25-27; Isaiah 40:4; 1 Timothy 1:17; Revelations 1:8, 4:8.
Sovereign and Creator	As the Creator and sustainer of life, God is sovereign; He is in control and has the right over the fate of His creation.	Exodus 3: 14-15; Psalm 16:2; 115:3.
Omniscient	God has perfect knowledge of all things. He is omniscient. God knows all past, present and future events. He knows the depths of the human heart and the life of each person.	Deuteronomy 2:7; Job 37:16; Proverbs 2:5-7; Psalms 73:11; 81:14-15; 94:11; 104:24; 139:1-4; 147: 5; Matthew 11: 21; James 1:15.
Omnipotent	God is almighty. There is no limit to God's power, and He can do anything He wants; there is nothing impossible for God.	Job 37:23; Jeremiah 32:17; Psalm 33:8-9.
Unchanging	God does not change. God is not capricious, but constant in His love and His purpose for salvation.	Malachi 3:6.
Omnipresent	God is always present everywhere at the same time. He fills everything; nothing exists outside of His presence. There is no place on the earth, in the sea, in the sky or in hell where people can escape from God's presence. Only God has this attribute; Satan, the angels and demons are not omnipresent.	Jeremiah 23:24; Psalm 139:7-12.
Spirit	God does not have a physical body; He is a spirit and is invisible to our eyes.	John 4:24; Colossians 1:15; 1 Timothy 1:17; Hebrews 11:27.

Alpha and Omega are the first and last letters of the Greek alphabet, so when God says that He is Alpha and Omega it means that He is before all else and is after everything else, that is, He is the beginning of everything and always will be the end of everything.

*The name Jehovah is derived from the Hebrew word hyh or hwh (to be), and is translated as "He is." This name refers to the eternity and autonomy of God over creation.
It also means
"One who gives life."*

What Is God's Character Like?

The Bible reveals the one true God.

God is a person with a character full of exceptional and outstanding qualities that He wants to share with His children.

The Old Testament says that God is holy (in Hebrew, qadosh). This holiness is not just one of His qualities, but it constitutes His essential character (Leviticus 19:2, Exodus 15:1, Psalm 22:3, John 17:11). This means you can call God "holy" in the same way that we call Him God, for "holy is his name" (Isaiah 57:15, Luke 1:49, Revelation 4:8).

God is the only being that is holy in and of Himself (Isaiah 6:1-7). The Old Testament also describes as holy some places, objects and people that were dedicated to God's service. For example, the Sabbath is a holy day because it has been set apart by the Lord (Genesis 2:3, Exodus 20:8). Mount Zion was holy, because it was there that God appeared to Moses (Psalm 2:6).

The word Adonai in Hebrew means Lord, master or owner. The Bible says that God owns everything and therefore has the right to demand unconditional obedience of all human beings.

God is the creator and sustainer of all in the universe and seeks to communicate with the creatures that live in the cosmos. God has not abandoned His creation (deist teaching), nor has he left it to drift, so that everything happens as a result of the natural evolution (as evolutionists claim), neither is He distributed in energy particles forming part of His creation (as pantheists or New Agers believe).

The priests were holy because God had set them apart for that office (Exodus 28:41).

When the Bible says that God is holy, it means that God is perfect both ethically and morally, and that His qualities of justice, truth, loyalty and integrity are absolute and perfect. God wants His children to be holy and perfect in the same way (1 Peter 1:16, Matthew 5:48). The Holy Spirit produces this progressive holiness in the disciple of Christ, beginning at the moment of conversion and deepening this process with the fullness of the Spirit in sanctification (Philippians 3:12, Colossians 1:28).

While the Old Testament emphasizes the holiness of God, the New Testament emphasizes His love. 1 John 4:8 states that God is love, that is, love is the very essence of His being. The love of God is the force that moves this world and is the present power that motivates everything He does.

Although it seems contradictory, even his judgment and anger are the result of his love and are directed toward anything that damages his creatures. That is why the Word teaches that God hates sin but loves the sinner. God will always act in accordance with what is right and just; he will reward those who do good and punish those who do evil.

God sent his Son into the world to show his love and to teach his children to love as He loves. What are the characteristics of God's love? We find the answer to that question in 1 Corinthians 13:4-7.

The love that comes from God is...

1. Patient
2. Kind
3. Does not envy
4. Does not boast
5. Is not proud
6. Does not dishonor others
7. Is not self-seeking
8. Is not easily angered
9. Keeps no record of wrongs
10. Does not delight in evil
11. Always protects
12. Always trusts
13. Always hopes
14. Always perseveres

Christians are called to let this holy love of God grow deeper and deeper into their being. The goal of the Christian life is to be mature in loving God and our neighbor; to grow in this sort of love is to grow in holiness. The goal is to reach the fullness of love that was in Christ Jesus who showed us how to live in a way that is pleasing to the Father (Ephesians 4:15).

"Hear, O Israel: The Lord our God, the Lord is one." This is a clear statement of monotheism; there is only one God, and that God is one. He is one; there is no other God (Deuteronomy 6:4 NIV).

WHAT DID WE LEARN?

Theology helps us to know what the Bible teaches about the true God, the creator and sustainer of life and the ruler of the universe so we can differentiate Him from other "gods" created by human beings. God is one, but He has revealed himself in three persons: Father, Son and Holy Spirit. God is a God of holy love that longs to rescue people from the destructive power of sin and to bring them into joyful communion with Him.

INSTRUCTIONS:

1. Develop a list of some idols that people have today.

_____
_____
_____
_____

2. In groups of three, choose one of the attributes of God and select an image or illustration from your context that could be useful to describe this attribute of God to non-Christian people in a simple and visual way.

_____
_____
_____
_____

3. In your own words, write a five line personal reflection on this topic: "Our God is a God of holy love."

_____
_____
_____
_____
_____

4. In groups of three or four, discuss and then propose a solution for the following case study:

"Tony is an 18 year old new Christian who studies at the university. Several of his teachers have said that God does not exist, and that He is just something that people have invented. The Chemistry professor, for example, insists that such a thing as God cannot exist, arguing that his existence cannot be verified. He also says that if God did exist there would be no hunger, poverty, injustice, hatred, wars, etc. in this world. Tony is confused and has begun to doubt the existence of God."

What would you say to Tony to help affirm his belief in the existence of God?

_____
_____
_____
_____

WHAT IS THE BIBLE?

Objectives

- To understand the origins of the Scriptures.
- To explain the inspiration of the Bible.
- To value the Bible for its transforming power.

Main Ideas

- The Bible is the book through which God speaks to His children.
- The Holy Spirit guided the biblical authors to convey the message of God to His people.
- The daily study of the Bible nourishes Christian life.

Introduction

The Bible is a collection of 66 books written by over 40 authors. Among the various authors are kings, prophets, shepherds, craftsmen, fishermen, soldiers, poets, a doctor, government ministers and many others who were inspired and guided by the Spirit of God.

Some of these authors wrote more than 1500 years ago. However, the correspondence and unity of message among them is extraordinary in spite of the fact that most of them did not get to meet each other in person.

There is no other book like the Bible, which is inspired by God and can fully satisfy all human needs.

How Was the Bible Written?

"We believe in the plenary inspiration of the Holy Scriptures, by which we understand the 66 books of the Old and New Testaments, given by divine inspiration, inerrantly revealing the will of God concerning us in all things necessary to our salvation, so that whatever is not contained therein is not to be enjoined as an article of faith."
(Luke 24:44-47; John 10:35; 1 Corinthians 15:3-4; 2 Timothy 3:15-17; 1 Peter 1:10-12; 2 Peter 1:20-21) (Article of Faith No. 4, Manual of the Church of the Nazarene 2009-2013).

In this section you will get to know the story of the origins of the Bible.

From earliest times God commanded his people to spread the message of Jesus by all means possible to their children and grandchildren so that they could get to know God's will and live according to it (Deuteronomy 6:6-9).

The books of the Bible were written at God's command. Moses gathered the stories of his ancestors, now found in the book of Genesis. These narratives had been passed down orally or on clay tablets. Archaeology has confirmed that writing was used more than 1,000 years before Abraham (Hebrews 9:19; Deuteronomy 27:2-8).

The books of the Bible were originally written in several languages:

Hebrew: Almost all the 39 books of the Old Testament were written in Hebrew. The Israelites learned Hebrew from the Semitic peoples living in Canaan at the time of Abraham.

Aramaic: Portions of Daniel and Ezra were written in Aramaic. The Jewish people learned Aramaic during their captivity in Babylon. It became the common language and was spoken by Jesus. Matthew wrote his gospel in Aramaic, but then it was translated into Greek.

Greek: Most of the books of the New Testament were written in Greek. At the time of Jesus, all the writings of the Old Testament had been translated into Greek since this was the common language that was used in the countries of the Roman Empire.

We can thank God that the Bible has been translated and published in hundreds of languages, and we have access to it in our own language.

The Word of God Was Inspired by the Holy Spirit

We believe that the entire Bible is the Word of God.

The text in 2 Peter 1:19-21 states: *"We also have the prophetic message as something completely reliable, and you will do well to pay attention to it, as to a light shining in a dark place, until the day dawns and the morning star rises in your hearts. Above all, you must understand that no prophecy of Scripture came about by the prophet's own interpretation of things. For prophecy never had its origin in the human will, but prophets, though human, spoke from God as they were carried along by the Holy Spirit."*

In analyzing these words of Peter, we can understand that there was no doubt in his mind that we have the actual message from God. The authenticity of the Scriptures of the Old Testament as the Word of God can easily be checked by the fact that all the prophecies about the Messiah were fulfilled in the life of Jesus Christ.

Peter also says that the Word of God came not from the will of man, but instead by divine origin. He uses the Greek verb fero, meaning to carry or bring. The use of this verb indicates that the authors were moved along or compelled by the Holy Spirit, not acting in accordance with their own wills and expressing their own thoughts, but following God's mind in words given and ministered by Him" (Vine, 1999: 459).

In 2 Timothy 3:16 Paul also says: *"All Scripture is God-breathed and is useful for teaching, rebuking, correcting and training in righteousness."* The word inspiration is translated from the Greek adjective theopneustos, which literally means "breath of God." The people of New Testament times associated the way the Holy Spirit acts with the moving of the wind, since in both cases they are invisible, although it is possible to feel their presence and see their effects.

The word "inspired" means that the Holy Spirit was present with the biblical authors in a special and miraculous way revealing truths not known before, guiding and directing their thoughts to choose the right words to express the message they had received from God.

The Church of the Nazarene believes that the entire Bible is the Word of God; the authors were "inspired" by God, that is, they were guided by God

The Hebrew verb that translates to write means "cleave or break" and refers to the method of cuneiform writing, which later evolved into the letters of the alphabet. Science has identified 600 different signs in cuneiform.

In the time from Abraham to Moses, writing was done by using a blunt reed or a stylus that left "marks" or "wedges" on clay tablets which were then dried and hardened for preservation. This type of writing is called cuneiform.

Himself, to provide the necessary knowledge about the Creator for human beings so that people can live in obedience and fellowship with Him. We believe also that God himself has provided this sure guide to enable us to live each day in holiness following Jesus' example.

Is the Bible Still Relevant for Modern Times?

We believe that the authority of the Bible is the same for all ages.

Because the biblical authors reported the message they received from God to the people of their times, some do not believe that the message of the Bible is relevant for the present day. But while times change, the will of God for human beings does not change, because God is the same yesterday, today and forever. Human beings can change, but the way of salvation that God has revealed in the Bible for human beings never loses its validity.

Although the Bible presents the Word of God, not all Christians accept its authority as the only standard for life. There are churches that give this authority for Christian faith and conduct to other sources such as these:

✓ Individual and personal experiences.

✓ The collective experience or that gathered by generations of believers.

✓ Other authority figures, such as the opinions of church leaders or founders of a particular church.

For example, the Roman Catholic Church believes the word of the Popes has equal authority with the Bible. That is why they accept doctrines and practices which are not based on the biblical text, such as: the worship of dead saints, the ascension of Mary, among others. The same goes for groups like the Mormons or Jehovah's Witnesses, who put the ideas or teachings of their founders at the same level or even higher than the authority of Scripture.

The Church of the Nazarene and other Protestant churches accept the 66 books of the Bible as inspired by God. The Roman Catholic Church incorporates other books known as "apocryphal" or not inspired books.

Jesus and the Scriptures	
He obeyed them	He came to fulfill them: Matthew 5:17-20
He was guided by their plan	He fulfilled the prophecies about His life: Matthew 16:21-23
He subjected himself to the Father's plan of salvation	He fulfilled His mission as Savior: John 8:39-42
He fulfilled the ceremonial law	He practiced all that was expected of Him as a faithful Jew: Mark 14:16-18
He fulfilled the moral law	He became the perfect example: John 11:1-44

How Much Does a Christian Need to Know About the Bible?

The Bible aids the Christian in spiritual growth.

The Greek verb fero means to carry, to bring. The Greek adjective theopneustos, is the combination of two words: Theos, God and pneo, breathe. They are translated in our Bibles in English with words like inspired, guided or driven.

The Christian needs to study the Word of God thoroughly. When Christians neglect Bible reading, it slows their spiritual development. The reading and study of the Bible should be part of everyday Christian life rather than just opening the Word during church services.

The apostle Paul exhorts Timothy to be a dedicated student of the Word of God (2 Timothy 3:14-1) and this call is for every Christian. Each time a believer searches for God and opens the pages of his/her Bible, a connection is made with God. Reading the Bible is spiritual food: *"Man shall not live on bread alone, but on every word that comes from the mouth of God"* (Matthew 4:4).

The Word of God is powerful to teach and correct. The Bible guides us to live closer to God and further away from sin, makes us see when we are in the wrong, convicts us of sin and shows us that Jesus Christ is the only way to salvation. The Bible is extraordinarily powerful to give us knowledge of God and transform our lives. It is like a two-edged sword that penetrates the depths of the heart (2 Timothy 3:16). The Word of God corrects and prepares for every good work.

Opening the Bible is like opening the email program on our computers where God communicates His will to us.

Peter compares the Word of God with a lamp that gives light to guide us in thick darkness (2 Peter 1:19-21). There is a story about a captain who on a dark night was trying to guide his ship at sea. Suddenly the lookout warned him that he had seen a light ahead. The captain assumed that it was the light of another boat, and ordered the watchman to send a message to that ship to move aside because it was in his line of navigation. They replied through signals that they would not move, and that it was the captain who had to change the direction of his boat.

The Bible is God's love letter to us, showing us how to have intimate fellowship with Him through Jesus Christ.

The captain insisted that they should change their route because his ship was a decorated military vessel. The answer he received was: "No matter how many insignias your captain has, you must move, because the light that you are seeing is from a lighthouse."

Like a lighthouse, the Word of God remains and no one has the right to modify it at will. It does not change. No negotiating with sin or sinful behavior is justified. People need to be transformed in accordance with the Lord's commands.

For Christians, the Bible is the most important book in the world as it communicates God's plan for the life and ministry of the church.

How Can I Hear God's Voice in the Bible?

"" Jesus answered, "It is written: Man shall not live on bread alone, but on every word that comes from the mouth of God" (Matthew 4:4).

The Bible contains the mind of God, the state of man, the way of salvation, the doom of sinners and the happiness of believers. Its doctrines are holy, its commandments are good and its stories are true. It is a source of wisdom for human beings; we must believe to be saved, and practice it to be holy. It contains light to guide us, food to sustain us, and comfort to encourage us.

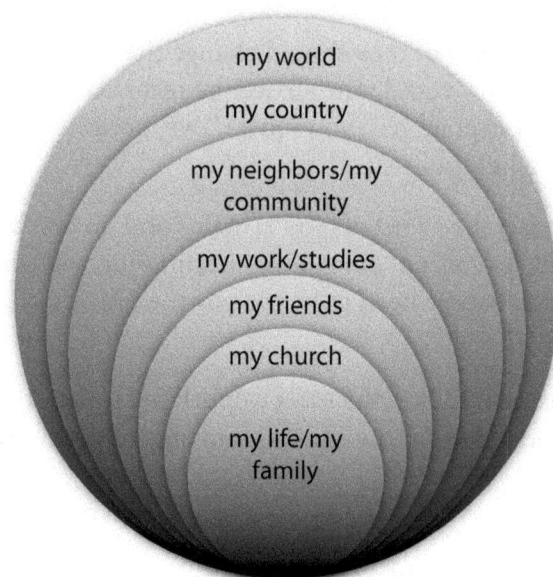

This section includes a simple method of Bible study.

Many Christians do not know how to study the Bible, and that is why we include in this lesson these simple steps:

1. Start praying that the Holy Spirit will speak through the portion of the Bible to be read.

2. Read the passage. It is advisable for new believers to start with one of the four Gospels (Matthew, Mark, Luke or John) and read a few verses each day.

3. While reading answer these questions:

- **What does it say?** To better understand the passage, you can read it in at least two versions. For example, you can use the New International Version, the Good News Translation, The Message, among others.

- **What does it mean?** Try to think what this message meant for the people who first heard it. To answer this question, if possible, it would be good to have on hand a Bible commentary and Bible dictionary.

- **What is God saying to me?** In answering this question, think of concentric circles. In the middle of the circle is your own life, then your family, friends, church, work or study, nearest neighbors, community, country and the world.

- **How I can start putting this into practice this week?** The Christian grows in the likeness of Christ not only from hearing God's voice, but also from putting into practice what has been learned.

my world
my country
my neighbors/my community
my work/studies
my friends
my church
my life/my family

School of Leadership - Principles of the Christian Life

Today there are many resources that can help us to understand the message that God left for his children in the Bible. Every Christian can gradually acquire at least two versions of the Bible, with one of them in simple language; a good Biblical commentary (preferably published by Wesleyans or Nazarenes); a Bible dictionary and an English dictionary. On the Internet there are also valuable resources of this type.

The time devoted to the study of the Bible is our best investment.

"The Bible will keep you from sin, or sin will keep you from the Bible." (D. L. Moody)

WHAT DID WE LEARN?

The entire Bible is the Word of God, written by authors inspired by Him. Through the Bible, God speaks to his children, showing them the way of salvation, teaching them how to live in holiness in the likeness of his Son Jesus Christ and calling them to serve others.

Activities

INSTRUCTIONS:

1. Explain in a way that a child could understand how the Bible is inspired by God.

_____

2. If someone asks you, "How can we be sure that the Bible is truly the Word of God?" what would be your answer?

_____

_____

_____

_____

3. In addition to individual or family Bible study, mention other ways in which we can learn from the Word through the ministries of the church.

_____

_____

_____

_____

4. Read Psalm 1: 1-3 and write a comment explaining how to apply the words of the psalmist to your life: "...whose delight is in the law of the Lord, and who meditates on his law day and night."

_____

_____

_____

_____

5. In groups of three or four people, share experiences of how the Holy Spirit has spoken or led at a specific time of your life through the Bible.

_____

_____

_____

_____

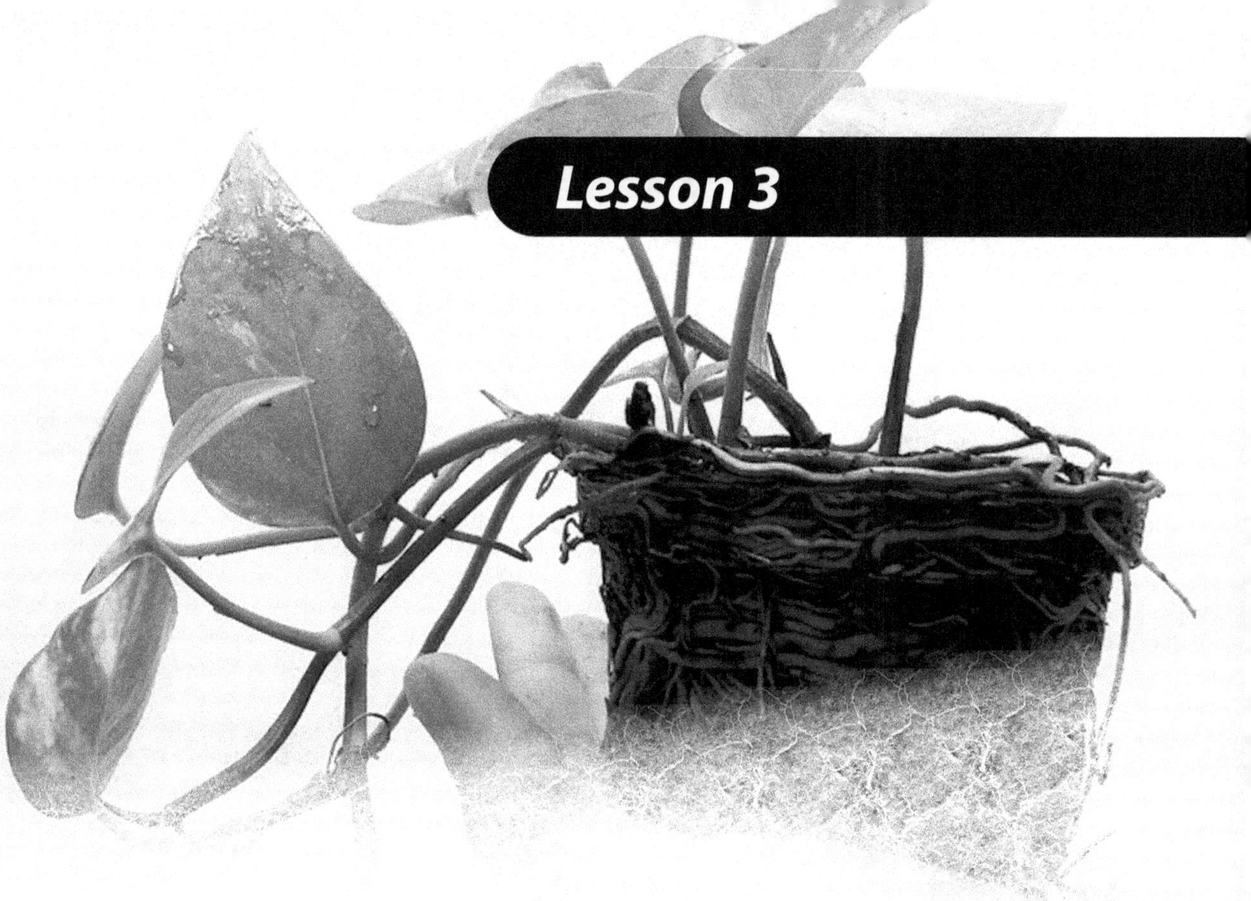

Lesson 3

Who Is Jesus?

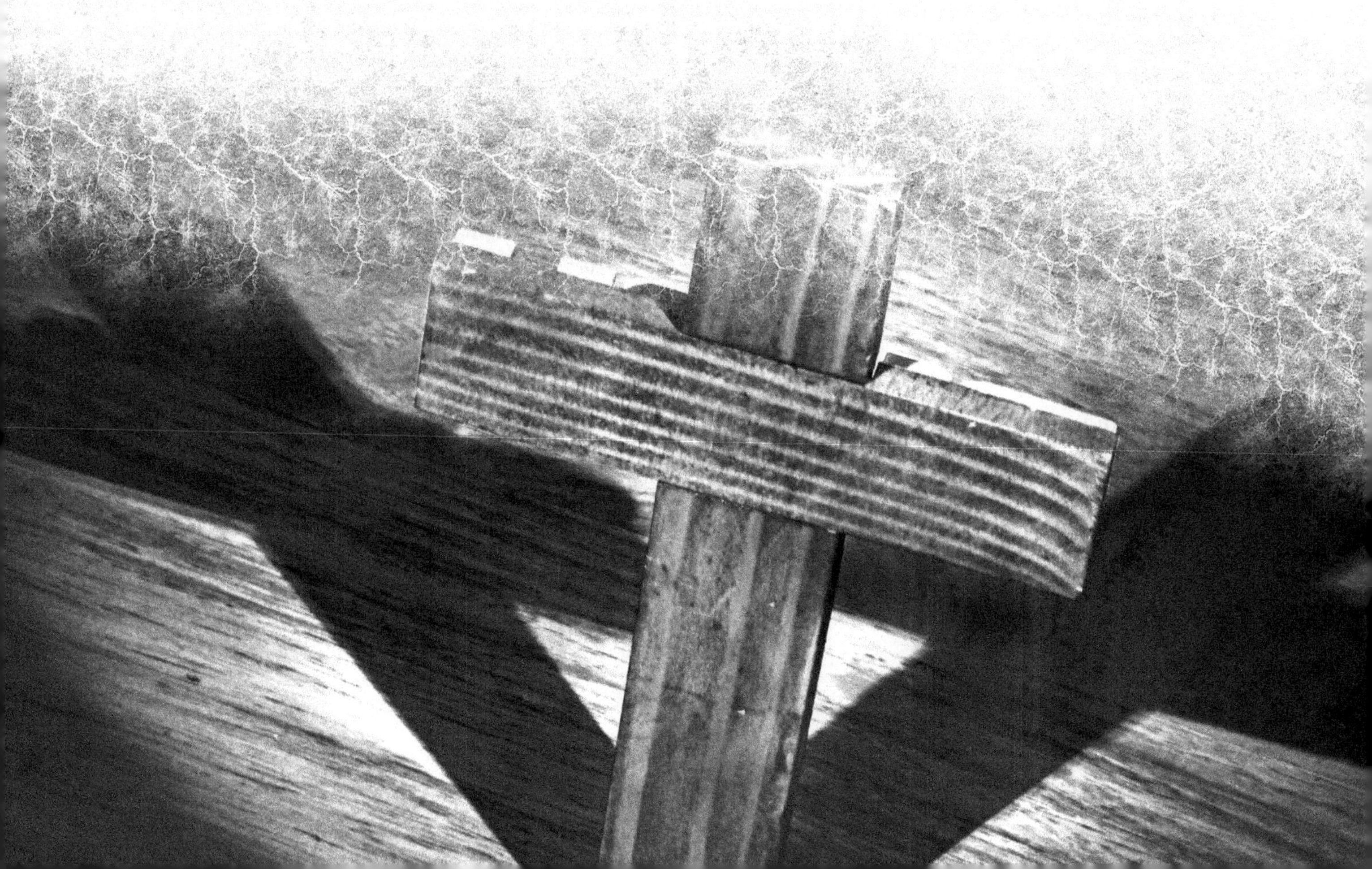

Objectives

- To understand the dual nature of Jesus: human and divine.
- To understand Jesus' role as Savior, Lord and Healer.

Main Ideas

- In the incarnation, Jesus Christ, the second person of the Trinity, took on human form.
- In Jesus Christ, the divine and human natures coexisted completely and perfectly.
- Jesus Christ is the only Savior and Lord. He has the power to forgive and heal.

Only begotten: only child

"Christos" is the Greek name for Messiah in Hebrew and refers to the divine nature of God's eternal Son. Jesus, which means Savior, is the name that indicates His human incarnate nature. Therefore, it is correct to refer to the Son of God as Jesus Christ, as that name indicates his dual divine and human natures.

Introduction

Faith in Jesus Christ is the distinctive belief of Christianity, but not everyone accepts the Christ revealed in the Bible. For example, Jehovah's Witnesses do not believe in the divinity of Christ, and the Mormons deny that Jesus Christ was conceived by the Holy Spirit. These are examples of misconceptions about Jesus circulating in our communities.

Nazarenes confess that Jesus is the Son of God who came to rescue the world from the power of sin. This act restores people's communion with God. Jesus' mission was not only to alleviate people's problems and sufferings, but also to resolve the issue of the root of evil that dwells in the human heart.

The second Article of Faith of the Church of the Nazarene states:

"We believe in Jesus Christ, the Second Person of the Triune Godhead; that He was eternally one with the Father; that He became incarnate by the Holy Spirit and was born of the Virgin Mary, so that two whole and perfect natures, that is to say the Godhead and manhood, are thus united in one Person very God and very man, the God-man. We believe that Jesus Christ died for our sins, and that He truly arose from the dead and took again His body, together with all things appertaining to the perfection of man's nature, wherewith He ascended into heaven and is there engaged in intercession for us."

(Matthew 1:20-25; 16:15-16; Luke 1:26-35; John 1:1-18; Acts 2:22-36; Romans 8:3, 32-34; Galatians 4:4-5; Philippians 2:5-11; Colossians 1:12-22; 1Timothy 6:14-16; Hebrews 1:1-5; 7:22-28; 9:24-28; 1 John 1:1-3; 4:2-3, 15) (Manual of the Church of the Nazarene, 2013-2017).

Jesus Christ Is God

In this section we will study the divine nature of Jesus.

The Bible declares that Jesus Christ is the eternal Word of God: *"In the beginning was the Word, and the Word was with God, and the Word was God"* (John 1:1). Christ existed eternally with the Father and the Spirit; in other words, before the Son of God was born as Jesus, He existed as God, and even when He was as a man He never ceased to be God (John 8:58).

Jesus taught that He is one with the Father (John 17:21) and He agreed to be called the "Son of God" (Matthew 14:33, John 9:38, Hebrews 2:9). In his writings, the Apostle Paul emphasizes the deity of Christ, refuting the teaching of the Greek philosophers of his time claiming that the matter (the body) was evil and the spirit was good and that it was therefore not possible that God could dwell in a human body (Colossians 1:15-22; 2:2,3,9). Jesus was not only fully God but also fully human.

The Humanity of Jesus Christ

We owe our salvation to the fact that Christ Jesus humbled himself completely.

Jesus was born of a virgin who was conceived by the Holy Spirit (Matthew 1:25). Jesus' birth is a unique, unrepeatable event in history; it is the miracle of incarnation.

The apostle Paul writes in Philippians 2:5-8 (NIV), *"In your relationships with one another, have the same mindset as Christ Jesus: Who, being in very nature of God, did not consider equality with God something to be used to his own advantage; rather, he made himself nothing by taking the very nature of a servant, being made in human likeness. And being found in appearance as a man, he humbled himself by becoming obedient to death—even death on a cross!"*

Jesus did not resort to his divine privileges, but "made himself nothing," putting his privileges aside in order to fulfill the mission entrusted to him by his Father. The divine Creator chose to share in the inferior nature of those He created; that is, He gave up his divine privileges to become one of us.

When Jesus "put aside his divine privileges," he did not give up his divine origin and identity, but he took the path of an obedient servant of the Father, knowing that obedience would ultimately lead to the cross of Calvary. Therefore, when Jesus "made himself nothing," he identified himself with the pain, feelings and sufferings that are part of human existence.

Also we need to remember that Jesus did not come to a rich man's home where he could enjoy wealth and power, but he was born into a poor family

Original sin: the inherited condition that lies in the human heart that drives a person to live in a selfish manner, satisfying his or her own desires and whims. Every Christian needs to be cleansed of this condition by the filling of the Holy Spirit (Ephesians 2:3).

When the Scriptures say Jesus "became flesh" it means that He "adopted" human nature. That is, the Son of God, infinite and eternal, became finite; the invisible became visible and palpable, and the Eternal was limited to time and the Supernatural reduced Himself to the natural. The Bible teaches that false teachers and false religions are those who deny the incarnation of Jesus Christ (John 1:14, 6:51,55).

Atonement: the act of paying someone else's debt. This is what Jesus did by dying on the cross; He suffered the punishment that our sin deserved according to the righteousness of God. To settle our debt, He made us free from the power of sin and death. It is only through voluntary surrender that we may be called children of God and receive the gift of eternal life (2 Corinthians 5:19, Hebrews 2:17).

Redeem means to buy back something that was lost.

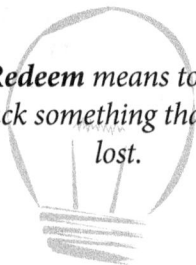

"Salvation is found in no one else, for there is no other name under heaven given to mankind by which we must be saved" (Acts 4:12).

(Luke 2). In this way, He identified with humanity and knew the pain and deprivation of the poor. The Gospels state that Jesus experienced all kinds of needs: he was hungry, thirsty and tired. He also slept, wept, and suffered pain, rejection, weakness and physical death (Matthew 4:2, John 4:6, 12:27, Isaiah 53:3-5, 1 Peter 3:18).

Thanks to Christ's obedience, salvation is made possible. Jesus Christ is the ultimate example of humility, obedience and self-denial.

Jesus Christ shared completely in human nature, with the exception of sin (2 Corinthians 5:21). There was no original sin in him, and He did not commit any sins (1 Peter 2:22).

Jesus Is Our Savior

Jesus Christ is the only way to the Father.

The Bible says *"God was reconciling the world to himself in Christ"* (2 Corinthians 5:19). The name "Jesus Christ" expresses the unique nature of His mission. It is the union of two words: Jesus and Christ. Christ is the Greek word for Messiah, while the Hebrew word Jesus means Savior. Jesus is the perfect Lamb (without defects) sent by God for sacrifice (atonement) to save humanity from the deserved punishment for sin that cannot be hidden from God's eyes; the punishment is death and eternal separation from the Creator.

In John 3:16-21, we find a summary statement of the purpose of God in sending his only Son into the world.

1. God's character: *"For God so loved…"* (3:16), teaches that the origin and the initiative of salvation come from God's love for human beings. His love is full of understanding, tenderness and mercy.

2. The object of God's love: *" God so loved the world..."* shows the extent of God's love. God loved the world and no person is excluded (Isaiah 45:22). We are the object of God's love. Thanks be to God!

3. The gift of God's love: *"he gave his one and only Son..."* The Father gave his only Son, the one whom he loved so much, to regain His lost children so that they might have eternal life.

4. The purpose of God's love: *"that whoever believes in him shall not perish but have eternal life."* There are two important aspects of God's love here. First, the Lord is not willing that anyone should perish. This shows that He has not abandoned humanity. Secondly, the main manifestation of God's love is through Jesus Christ, so that everyone who believes in Him and accepts Him as Savior has eternal life.

The Bible declares that Jesus Christ is the only way of salvation provided by God for mankind. So what does it mean to believe in Jesus?

- To accept God's love.

- To believe that God sent Jesus Christ to save us through his death and resurrection.

- To accept Jesus as Savior and Lord.

- To follow Jesus as his disciples.

- To completely submit our wills in obedience to Christ with no excuses.

When the Bible speaks of believing, it refers not just to intellectual knowledge, but rather to a lifestyle. It is not the same sort of believing we experience with one of the heroes in the history of our country. Neither is it the occasional faith we put in Jesus when we need Him to perform a miracle. It is putting all our trust in Jesus Christ and giving Him our lives and placing our future into his hands. This form of believing will be seen in the way we live each day as we follow Jesus.

The Bible teaches that those who reject the Son of God and do not believe in Him are condemned by their own choice. All people are free to accept or reject the invitation of the Lord and Savior (John 3:17-21). The decision is an individual one.

Jesus Is Lord of Lords

God exalted Jesus Christ as the highest authority in the universe.

The apostle Paul also speaks of the exaltation of Christ: "*Therefore God exalted him to the highest place and gave him the name that is above every name, that at the name of Jesus every knee should bow, in heaven and on earth and under the earth, and every tongue acknowledge that Jesus Christ is Lord, to the glory of God the Father*" (Philippians 2:9-11).

To exalt means to raise up a person or thing in status or dignity. After spending three days in the tomb, the risen Jesus appeared to the disciples and was with them for forty days. After that, He ascended to his Father and in this way He ended his ministry on earth. By raising Jesus from the dead, the Father highly exalted Him, but what does this exaltation mean?

Paul says that God gave Him a name that is above every name. This is difficult to understand. How important can a change of name be? In our social context, when we name our children, we might look at a list of names, ask for suggestions or give the child the name of one of our loved ones. But in Eastern cultures, naming a child was of paramount importance because the name should express the character of that person. Verses 10 and 11 convey this idea about the Lord Jesus; His name is above every name. There is no greater authority than that of Jesus Christ in the universe!

This new name describes Jesus' true divine nature and His place over all creation, including over spiritual beings, people and other creatures. This

To study about Jesus Christ and his redemptive work, refer to these Scriptures:
John 3:16-21
Philippians 2:5-11
Luke 4:16-30, 9:1-6
Matthew 20:29-34
Acts 9:32–35

And being found in appearance as a man, he humbled himself by becoming obedient to death — even death on a cross! Therefore God exalted him to the highest place and gave him the name that is above every name, that at the name of Jesus every knee should bow, in heaven and on earth and under the earth, and every tongue acknowledge that Jesus Christ is Lord, to the glory of God the Father (Philippians 2:8-11).

name is equivalent to that given to God in the Old Testament as sovereign King (Isaiah 45:21-23, Acts 2:34,36). The Bible says that all things were created by Him and for Him, and in Him all things hold together; He is Lord of the dead and of the living (Romans 14:6-9, Colossians 1:16-17). Jesus Christ owns and controls everything that exists. God's will is that everyone should recognize Jesus Christ as Lord.

Jesus Christ the Healer

Jesus Christ carried our pain on the cross.

Illness and death were never part of the original plan of the Creator for His creation, but they came as a result of human sin. The sacrifice of Jesus Christ on the cross of Calvary brought not only forgiveness, but also provides healing (Isaiah 53:4-5). There will be no disease, pain or death in Heaven (Revelations 22:2).

Jesus had compassion for the sick. He saw illness as an opportunity to show the glory and compassion of God. At the same time, He awakened in people their interest in hearing the good news of salvation (Matthew 4:23). He gave this example to the Church.

In Luke 9:1-6 and Acts 9:32-35, we can see the disciples ministering, continuing the work of Jesus Christ. They preached the message of the Kingdom of Heaven, but also cared for peoples' physical and emotional needs. Wherever they served, the presence of Jesus Christ - His love, His mercy and power-was with them.

All Christians have spiritual authority to pray with faith and compassion for the sick. God can also heal through medical science. When someone becomes sick, in addition to prayer, they need to visit a doctor as soon as possible, praying that God will guide the doctors in their treatment.

When a person is healed, he or she needs to be encouraged to testify to their family, friends and the church since many people can come to believe in Jesus through the testimony of someone who has been healed (James 5:13-15).

"Surely he took up our pain and bore our suffering, yet we considered him punished by God, stricken by him, and afflicted. But he was pierced for our transgressions, he was crushed for our iniquities; the punishment that brought us peace was on him, and by his wounds we are healed" (Isaiah 53:4-5).

People also need to learn to accept God's will, whatever it may be, as God does not heal everyone. Sometimes God allows sickness and physical weakness. Sometimes He reveals the reason why He allows this suffering, but if not, we can be confidant that there is a holy purpose to what God allows in our lives. In these cases, the believer can rest in God's special promise that He will help his sons and daughters to overcome trials (Romans 8:28, 2 Corinthians 12:7-10).

The Church of the Nazarene believes that God is the source of physical healing and that it is not His will that people suffer because of illness. As Nazarenes we believe in the biblical doctrine of divine healing and encourage our members to seek opportunities to pray in faith for the sick.

We also believe that God uses medical science and professionals to bring relief to suffering.

The Church must seek opportunities to minister to the sick, the afflicted and the oppressed. We also have a responsibility to help prevent diseases, teaching people to live healthy lives, caring for the spirit, mind, emotions and body.

Divine healing: physical healing that takes place miraculously, instantly or progressively and that comes from the hand of God. This healing occurs in response to believers' prayers of faith when it is God's will (John 4:46-53).

Gift of healing: supernatural ability given by the Holy Spirit to some Christians for the purpose of glorifying God.

WHAT DID WE LEARN?

Jesus Christ is the Son of God incarnate, sent by God to bring salvation, eternal life, restoration of fellowship with Him, and adoption into His family (the Church). Through His sacrifice, we can be cleansed from all sin and be healed.

1. In your own words answer the question: Who is Jesus?

_____

_____

_____

_____

2. Why is it so important to believe in the divinity of Jesus Christ?

_____

_____

_____

_____

3. What does it mean for Christians to accept Jesus Christ as Savior and Lord?

_____

_____

_____

_____

4. Some people believe that God is responsible for human pain and suffering. What answer would you give them?

_____

_____

_____

_____

5. In groups of three or four, identify the most common diseases of people in your community and think of some ways your church could help prevent or alleviate these ailments.

_____

_____

_____

_____

WHO IS THE HOLY SPIRIT?

- To know the Holy Spirit.
- To value the Spirit's work in spiritual growth.
- To understand that the Church needs the guidance of the Spirit in its mission.

Main Ideas

-The Holy Spirit is the third person of the Holy Trinity.
-Jesus sent the Spirit to give us new life and teach us how to live in holiness.
-The Holy Spirit guides the ministry and mission of the Church in the world.

Introduction

What was the work of the Holy Spirit in creation according to Genesis 1?

The Holy Spirit is vital for growth and Christian maturity. In this lesson we will study the ministry of the Holy Spirit in our midst.

The Holy Spirit is a real person who came to live in Jesus' true followers after He rose from the dead and ascended into heaven (John 14:16-18). He is God in the same way as God the Father and God the Son, and the Spirit has all the same divine qualities.

The Spirit's main function is to bear witness to people about the truth revealed in the life and teachings of Jesus (John 15:26, 16:14). The Holy Spirit also acts as the Christians' teacher, revealing the will and the truth of God (1 Corinthians 2: 9-14). He is the living and active presence of God working in the world, but He especially works in ministry to the Church.

"We believe in the Holy Spirit, the Third Person of the Triune Godhead, that He is ever present and efficiently active in and with the Church of Christ, convincing the world of sin, regenerating those who repent and believe, sanctifying believers, and guiding into all truth as it is in Jesus" (Article of Faith No. 3, Manual of the Church of the Nazarene 2009-2013).

The Coming of the Holy Spirit and His Work

In this section we will study why the Holy Spirit came.

The Lord Jesus taught His disciples about the ministry of the Holy Spirit in the Gospel of John chapter 16. This passage teaches us the following:

1. The physical absence of the Lord Jesus Christ was necessary. The disciples were sad. All they knew was that their teacher was to going to leave them. However, Jesus said that this is the best thing that could happen because only then would the Holy Spirit come.

This meant that the work of the Holy Spirit would be even greater than that of Jesus. As a human being, Jesus was limited. He could not be, for example, with his followers in Galilee and Judea at the same time. The Holy Spirit would not be subject to those limitations, but would be able to be present with Jesus' disciples anywhere and at anytime.

2. The coming of the Holy Spirit would be the fulfillment of the promise of Jesus Christ. Before ascending to His Father, Jesus Christ left His disciples a Great Commission, but He also said, *"...And surely I am with you always, to the very end of the age"* (Matthew 28:20 NIV). This promise would come true only through the Holy Spirit. Moreover, this presence would strengthen the faith of the disciples and give them power and authority to make disciples of Christ in all nations.

3. The Holy Spirit will convict the world of sin, righteousness and judgment. Of sin, because the Holy Spirit convicts people of their sin and brings them to Christ; of righteousness, because the Holy Spirit makes us understand that we can only obtain God's forgiveness through Jesus Christ; of judgment, because the Holy Spirit allows us to be forgiven of the punishment our sins deserve on the day of the judgment of God by showing us the way of salvation and forgiveness through Jesus Christ and reconciling us to God.

In conclusion, without the ministry of the Holy Spirit, humanity itself could never find forgiveness from God and attain reconciliation with God through Jesus Christ. In other words, we would be hopelessly condemned to live in the bondage of sin, far away from the love of our Creator.

To study about the Holy Spirit, refer to these Scriptures:
Joel 2:28-32
John 14:15-26, 16:7-13
Acts 15:8-9
2 Thessalonians 2:13
1 Peter 1:12

The Holy Spirit, Our Helper

The Holy Spirit assists, rescues and helps us.

In John 14:15-26 Jesus taught about some special functions of the ministry of the Holy Spirit in the believer's life.

The following is a contemporary adaptation of the passage in John 14:15-17 as a "letter from Jesus to one of his disciples." It clearly explains the ministry of the Holy Spirit as our helper, comforter and counselor:

Dear disciple:

You know that I have to go. When I said I was returning to my Father, I saw your face and I realized that your heart was sad. But, listen to me. I do it for your own good. I'd like to spend more time with you, but if I do not go, you will not receive the help you will need from now on.

I know you love me. Therefore, keep in your heart everything I have taught you. But do not forget something important; just as I was obedient to the Father, so should you be. The Holy Spirit, whom I will send, is the person who will help you to be obedient to God and at the same time to remember everything I have taught you. When the Holy Spirit comes to you, He will give you power and authority to fulfill the ministry entrusted to you.

Another reason that I must go to my Father is to prepare the place where you will live forever. It is the same place where I will live. But to enjoy this place, you have to be obedient to the Father in everything. When that time comes, I will find you and be with you.

As the Comforter, the Holy Spirit comforts us, encourages us and makes us stronger.

"The Holy Spirit guides us into all truth and Jesus" (Leonard Gay)

I don't want you to be sad, because I'll be praying to the Father to send the Holy Spirit to be with you and with all those who love me. I'm sorry for those who ignore or reject me because they will not have the promises that you will enjoy, nor will they receive the Holy Spirit. Remember the teachings I gave you; trust me, I will not disappoint you.

Regarding the Holy Spirit whom I will send, He already knows about you, your love for the Father, your struggles and your desires. He will help you, especially to be obedient in everything. Be encouraged!

Your Teacher and Friend, Jesus Christ

The Holy Spirit, the Helper, will always be alongside Christians to help them to keep the teachings of Jesus Christ and to be faithful and obedient to God the Father.

The Holy Spirit, Our Teacher

As a teacher, the Spirit teaches us to live in holiness just as Christ did.

In John 14:18-24, Jesus said He would not leave His disciples as orphans, but would be present with them through the Holy Spirit. Later in John 14:25-26, Jesus describes the ministry of the Holy Spirit as the Teacher.

When the Holy Spirit lives in the heart of a disciple or follower of Christ, He can guide the course of his/her life from then on. His ministry is to teach and direct every aspect of life in harmony with the will of God; He reveals the deep truths of the Word of God and helps to implement them in their daily lives.

The Holy Spirit also illuminates our minds and reminds us of the teachings of Jesus that we have studied in his Word. He also helps us live in holiness, guiding us to make decisions every day based on the principles and commandments of the Bible.

The Holy Spirit Gives Us Life

The Holy Spirit sustains the life of all living things in this world.

The Holy Spirit has the special task of giving life to all of creation on the planet. Psalm 104: 30 states: "When you send your Spirit, they are created, and you renew the face of the ground" (NIV). Job 34:14-15 says: "If it were his intention and he withdrew his spirit and breath, all humanity would perish together and mankind would return to the dust" (NIV). Without the presence of the Holy Spirit there would be no life on this planet.

Also, it is the Holy Spirit who gives new life to the believer in regeneration (John 3:5). When someone accepts Jesus as his or her personal

Savior, it is through the Holy Spirit that the person is born again as a new creature in Christ. Before, the person was spiritually dead, and the spirit was separated from God and had no eternal life. It is the Holy Spirit who "regenerates," or in other words, gives our spirit life, a life that comes from God and identifies us as members of God's family, His Church (Romans 8:2).

"And I will put my Spirit in you and move you to follow my decrees and be careful to keep my laws" (Ezekiel 36:27 NIV).

The Holy Spirit Gives Us Power to Serve

What kind of power does the Holy Spirit provide for the believer?

It is the Holy Spirit who equips believers to serve others (Acts 2:1-13). One of the ways in which the Spirit helps is by providing spiritual gifts, which are "special skills" or tools for church ministries. The Spirit gave authority to the 120 disciples gathered at Pentecost to carry out their ministries (Acts 1:8). They needed the Holy Spirit to take the message of salvation with courage and great power (Acts 4:8, 31, 6:10).

The apostle Paul wrote to the church at Corinth: *"There are different kinds of gifts, but the same Spirit distributes them. There are different kinds of service, but the same Lord. There are different kinds of working, but in all of them and in everyone it is the same God at work. Now to each one the manifestation of the Spirit is given for the common good. To one there is given through the Spirit a message of wisdom, to another a message of knowledge by means of the same Spirit, to another faith by the same Spirit, to another gifts of healing by that one Spirit, to another miraculous powers, to another prophecy, to another distinguishing between spirits, to another speaking in different kinds of tongues, and to still another the interpretation of tongues. All these are the work of one and the same Spirit, and he distributes them to each one, just as he determines"* (1 Corinthians 12: 4-11 NIV).

Regeneration is the translation of the Greek term "palingenesia" meaning new birth or born again, and refers to the inner transformation that the Holy Spirit carries out in the new believer (Titus 3:5). Other terms similar in meaning are used in Ephesians 2:1,5, James 1:18, 1 Peter 1:23.

These capabilities mentioned by Paul are some that the Spirit had distributed among the Christians of the church in Corinth. In every age and in every particular context, the Spirit distributes to the church the gifts that it needs to serve the people in its community. The gifts are never for personal gain, or so that some believers become more important than others, but they are given to help the church fulfill its mission. The gifts help us to serve in various ministries and church functions, so that each of the members can grow in Christlikeness and serve others according to their particular calling.

The Lord has a special ministry for each of his followers, for which He has given gifts of the Spirit and special abilities. God desires that all these resources be used responsibly and with humility in service to others.

The Ministry of the Holy Spirit in the Church

The initiative in regeneration is ascribed to God (Jn 1:13); it is from above (Jn 3:3,7) and of the Spirit (Jn 3:5, 8)….This divine act is decisive and once for all" (Marshall 1115).

How does the Holy Spirit guide the ministry of the Church?

Jesus told His disciples what the work of the Spirit would be in the world, in their lives and in the Church. In John 16:12-15, Jesus taught that the Holy Spirit would be with them every day and would direct them in their ministries.

The Scriptures confirm that this promise was fulfilled. We read in the book of Acts about the ministry of the Holy Spirit guiding the apostles in the early church. Without the presence of the Holy Spirit, the church would not have the power and authority to fulfill the ministry of preaching the gospel to all nations. There is no area in the life of the Church that does not require the presence, help and guidance of the Holy Spirit (Ephesians 3:14-21).

"Don't you know that your body is the temple of the Holy Spirit, who lives in you and who was given to you by God? You do not belong to yourselves but to God" (I Corinthians 6:19, Good News Bible).

More Teaching Concerning the Holy Spirit in John 14:16-17	
He comes from the father.	God is manifested through the Holy Spirit. Jesus declares that He has sent us out in the power of God.
He is a person.	He is not an "influence," "force" or "energy." He is a Divine Person to whom we owe respect and adoration. He is a Holy Person who has come to dwell in our lives.
He remains with us continually until Christ returns.	The Holy Spirit has come to stay with us until the end of all time.
He is the Spirit of Truth.	He is called "the Spirit of truth" because He is the one who inspired the Scriptures and it is He who leads the believer to understand its message (2 Peter 1:21).
He is not in everyone.	The Spirit of God can only dwell in those who have received new life in Christ.
He lives with and in us.	This distinction is important. He not only helps us every day, but He is also in us as Lord of our lives. Our bodies become, by divine grace, the temple of the Spirit of God.

The Fruit of the Spirit

- Love
- Peace
- Joy
- Patience
- Kindness
- Self-Control
- Goodness
- Gentleness
- Faithfulness

The Holy Spirit Acting in the Early Church
- He led them to recognize the truth: Acts 5:3
- He led them to choose leaders: Acts 6:3-5, 13:2, 20:28
- He give them strength to stand strong during martyrdom: Acts 7:55
- He strengthened new churches: Acts 9:31
- He led them to new mission fields: Acts 13:4, 16:6

WHAT DID WE LEARN?

The Holy Spirit is a divine person. His ministry to the believer and the church is essential. He gives new spiritual life at the time of conversion and guides the believer in the process of becoming more like Christ. The Spirit also sanctifies the believer at the time of the filling of the Spirit; He calls and trains for service.

Activities

INSTRUCTIONS:

1. Answer in your own words this question: Who is the Holy Spirit?

_____

_____

_____

2. In the following list, put an "x" by those situations in which it is correct to ask for help from the Holy Spirit:

__ I am being tempted.

__ I am sad or discouraged.

__ I got up late because of laziness, and I have to arrive early to my job.

__ I am confused about a decision that I need to make.

__ I don't have enough time to complete all my responsibilities at home.

__ I struggle to give my tithe.

__ I didn't study for an exam.

__ I need to apologize to someone I have offended.

__ I know someone who is resisting accepting Jesus as their Savior.

__ I need to prepare to give a class or to preach.

3. After reading 1 Corinthians 6:19 and Ezekiel 36:27 answer the following question: For what purpose does God put His Spirit in His children?

_____

_____

_____

4. Make a list of all the things you do in a week. Do not forget to include rest, food, recreation, sharing with family, etc. Then evaluate each of them with the following question: In which of these activities am I using my life as a temple of the Holy Spirit?

_____

_____

_____

5. After praying a few minutes asking the Spirit's direction, examine your schedule of weekly activities. Are there some things that the Spirit is showing you that you need to remove from your life to make room for other things so that you can make better use of the temple of the Spirit, which is your body?

_____

_____

_____

WHY DO I NEED TO BE SAVED?

Objectives

- To value the origin and nature of human beings.
- To understand the meaning of sin.
- To understand God's plan to rescue human beings.

Main Ideas

- People are created by God, in His image and likeness.
- People are given the freedom to choose to do good or evil.
- God designed a plan of salvation by sending His Son to rescue us from sin so we can live in holiness.

Human beings bear the image of God in their spirit and soul.

God has devised a perfect plan for the salvation of mankind. Salvation is by grace; it is a gift of God, and there is nothing that man can do to deserve it or make it happen (Galatians 2:16, Ephesians 2:8-9).

Introduction

The Manual of the Church of the Nazarene, Article of Faith number 5, states the following about original and personal sin:

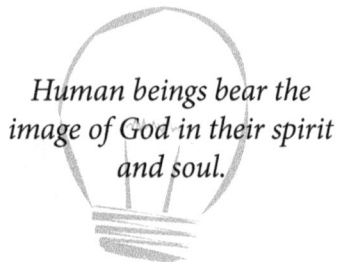

"We believe that sin came into the world through the disobedience of our first parents, and death by sin.

We believe that sin is of two kinds: original sin or depravity, and actual or personal sin. We believe that original sin, or depravity, is that corruption of the nature of all the offspring of Adam by reason of which everyone is very far gone from original righteousness or the pure state of our first parents at the time of their creation, is averse to God, is without spiritual life, and inclined to evil, and that continually.

We further believe that original sin continues to exist with the new life of the regenerate, until the heart is fully cleansed by the baptism with the Holy Spirit. We believe that original sin differs from actual sin in that it constitutes an inherited propensity to actual sin for which no one is accountable until it's divinely provided remedy is neglected or rejected.

We believe that actual or personal sin is a voluntary violation of a known law of God by a morally responsible person. It is therefore not to be confused with involuntary and inescapable shortcomings, infirmities, faults, mistakes, failures, or other deviations from a standard of perfect conduct that are the residual effects of the fall. However, such innocent effects do not include attitudes or responses contrary to the spirit of Christ, which may properly be called sins of the spirit. We believe that personal sin is primarily and essentially a violation of the law of love; and that in relation to Christ sin may be defined as unbelief.

(Original sin: Genesis 3; 6:5; Job 15:14; Psalm 51:5; Jeremiah 17:9-10; Mark 7:21-23; Romans 1:18-25; 5:12-14; 7:1-8:9; 1 Corinthians 3:1-4; Galatians 5:16-25; 1 John 1:7-8 Personal sin: Matthew 22:36-40 {with 1 John 3:4}; John 8:34-36; 16:8-9; Romans 3:23; 6:15-23; 8:18-24; 14:23; 1 John 1:9-2:4; 3:7-10)" (2013-2017).

The Church of the Nazarene affirms that the creation of the human race in the image of God included the ability to choose between good and evil and thus human beings were made morally responsible; that through the fall of Adam we all become sinners, so that now in our own strength or our own works, we cannot be free from sin and return to communion with God.

It also states that the grace of God through Jesus Christ is freely bestowed upon all people, enabling all who will to leave the life of sin, believe in Jesus Christ as Savior and Lord, receive pardon and cleansing from sin, and learn to live in holiness as disciples of the Lord.

We believe that a person who has been saved can fall back into a life of sin, if growth in the life of holiness is neglected. Unless the person repents and returns to a life of obedience to God, he or she will receive the same punishment as that prepared for sinners.

Origin and Nature of Human Beings

God created man holy in soul, body and spirit.

The creation story in Genesis rules out the scientific theories that place humanity as the highest level of an evolutionary process, and the idea that human beings are only different from other living things because they are more developed as animals or organisms.

The Bible states that God created the heavens and the earth and everything that exists, and as the crown of creation, God created mankind (Genesis 1:1-31). God said, *"Let us make man ..."* Here we notice the implied presence of the Divine Trinity devising the creation of human beings. God is in this initiative. He takes the dust of the earth to shape a new creature, in whom He can share His image. Genesis 2:7 says that God *"breathed the breath of life, and man became a living being."* God endowed man with qualities such as intelligence, will and emotions. Mankind was created morally good and sinless, with the ability to have a relationship of love and fellowship with the Creator.

Both Adam and Eve shared the image of God, but with some physical and emotional differences, so that they could complement each other, be helpmates for each other, fulfill God's command to reproduce, and exercise stewardship over the creation (Genesis 1:27,28).

The nature of man is composed of body, soul and spirit; these areas form a whole person and a single personality that cannot be divided. The physical body allows people to be in touch with the material world; the spirit will continue after the death of the physical body and allows one to have fellowship with the Spirit of God. The soul is the center of intellectual life, the emotions and the personality.

Salvation is the result of God's love for the world, but there is one condition. Whoever wishes to be saved must "believe" in Jesus Christ (John 3:16), and acknowledge and confess their sin: "If we confess our sins, he is faithful and just and will forgive us our sins and purify us from all unrighteousness" (1 John 1:9).

Atonement
"We believe that Jesus Christ, by His sufferings, by the shedding of His own blood, and by His death on the Cross, made a full atonement for all human sin, and that this Atonement is the only ground of salvation, and that it is sufficient for every individual of Adam's race. The Atonement is graciously efficacious for the salvation of [the irresponsible] those incapable of moral responsibility and for the children in innocency but is efficacious for the salvation of those who reach the age of responsibility only when they repent and believe" (Article of Faith No. 6, Manual of the Church of the Nazarene 2013-2017).

The Image of God in Mankind

Why did God give human beings capabilities and qualities in His image?

To study more about the Atonement:
Isaiah 53:5-6, 11, Mark 10:45, Luke 24:46-48, John 1:29, 3:14-17, Acts 4:10-12, Romans 3:21-26, 4:17 - 25, 5:6-21, 1 Corinthians 6:20, 2 Corinthians 5:14-21, Galatians 1:3-4, 3:13-14, Colossians 1:19-23, 1 Timothy 2:3-6; Titus 2:11-14, Hebrews 2:9, 9:11-14, 13:12, 1 Peter 1:18-21, 2:19-25, 1 John 2:1-2.

Psalm 8:5-6 speaks about the creation of human beings (Good News Translation): *"Yet you made them inferior only to yourself; you crowned them with glory and honor. You appointed them rulers over everything you made; you placed them over all creation."*

The fact that God crowned mankind with glory and honor indicates that He bestowed on them high dignity, as mentioned in Genesis 1:26-28. It implies that humans have been given the power to reign over the rest of creation here on earth, as well as being gifted with the ability to manage it.

Unfortunately, mankind chose to go against God, and therefore they "fall short of the glory of God" (Romans 3:23). This means that they lost their fellowship with the Creator. But God in His mercy allows human beings to administer creation, despite the destructive results that have resulted from mismanagement of natural resources. Planet Earth, the home that God gave us, is being destroyed by humans. If this irresponsible attitude continues, most likely in a few years we will live in a complete desert. The Christian has a responsibility to protect the environment and diligently worry about managing natural resources.

God declares that sinners are made right before His eyes, not on the basis of their good works, but in response to their faith in the work of Jesus Christ on the cross (Romans 4:5-8 and 5:1-5).

The Fall of Mankind

Where does the sinful nature of mankind start?

The disobedience of Adam and Eve permitted sin to enter their lives and this passed on to all their descendants. The image of God in them and the relationship with the Creator, the source of life, were both damaged. Their original nature was spoiled; they changed their state of purity for a sinful nature, which incites them to do evil (Romans 3:23).

When tempted by Satan, Adam and Eve rebelled against God and lost their holiness (2 Peter 2:4, Jude 6).

Olin A. Curtis, in "The Christian Faith," lists four items that occurred at the fall of the first couple in Genesis 3:1-6:

1. Physical appetite: Eve saw that the tree was good for food and pleasing to the eyes. Satan used the senses of the human body as a weakness to tempt.

2. Intellectual desire or "curiosity." The story tells us that the tree "was desirable because it could make someone wise." This curiosity refers to the impatient desire to experience new pleasures or emotions, demonstrating irresponsible and irrational behavior like that of a child.

3. The temptation included an individual impulse towards self-government: This question by the Devil demonstrates this temptation: "Is it true that God told you not to eat from any tree in the garden?" This is where the temptation comes to a critical point, because with this suggestion Satan induces the idea that human beings should not settle for a subordinate position in relationship to the higher authority of the Creator.

4. Social influence: Eve, after sinning, "gave to her husband, and he ate." Sin always causes suffering in the perpetrator and in those around them.

With the fall of man, sin enters the world: *"Therefore, just as sin entered the world through one man, and death through sin, and in this way death came to all people, because all sinned…"*(Romans 5:12). Sin comes to damage human life. Only the blood of Jesus Christ, shed on the cross of Calvary, can bring cleansing and forgiveness of sins.

The Bible says that every human being needs to be reconciled with his Creator, so that his or her holy nature might be restored, and communion with the living God can be recovered. This is only possible with the salvation that God has provided through His Son Jesus Christ (John 3:16).

God's Plan to Rescue Human Beings from Sin

God graciously provides the means for our salvation.

Salvation is the act by which man is reconciled to God. Everyone is born with a fallen nature, which inevitably leads us to disobey God. Only through the sacrifice of Jesus Christ can all acts of disobedience to God be forgiven, whether in thought, words or actions (Hebrews 9:14, 22). Jesus Christ made it possible for us to be reconciled to God, to become friends of God, and through adoption to return to the family of God as His children (Romans 5:10-11, 2 Corinthians 5:18-19).

It is by the Holy Spirit that God calls human beings to salvation; it is by the Spirit that we are convicted of sin and awakened to the awareness of our sin and our need for forgiveness. It is by the power of the Holy Spirit that people turn to God in repentance and faith. Also, it is through the Spirit that human beings are born a second time and are renewed in the image of God.

The work of the Holy Spirit in the world is what John Wesley describes as "prevenient grace." "Literally it means 'the grace that comes before' and refers to God's activity prior to any human movement toward God" (Dunning 338). This grace has an effect on the sinner enabling him or her to be willing to hear the good news of salvation, and to have the opportunity to decide to repent, believe in Jesus and be saved.

Prevenient Grace
"We believe that the human race's creation in Godlikeness included ability to choose between right and wrong, and that thus human beings were made morally responsible; that through the fall of Adam they became depraved so that they cannot now turn and prepare themselves by their own natural strength and works to faith and calling upon God. But we also believe that the grace of God through Jesus Christ is freely bestowed upon all people, enabling all who will to turn from sin to righteousness, believe on Jesus Christ for pardon and cleansing from sin, and follow good works pleasing and acceptable in His sight. We believe that all persons, though in the possession of the experience of regeneration and entire sanctification, may fall from grace and apostatize and, unless they repent of their sins, be hopelessly and eternally lost" (Article of Faith No. 7, Manual of the Church of the Nazarene 2013-2017).

Two people are involved in the process of salvation: God and mankind.

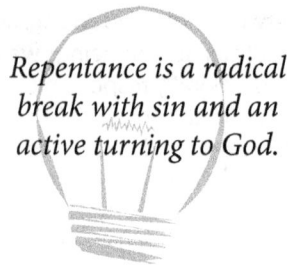

What people do	What God does
Repent (Acts 17:30)	Justifies: an act in which God grants full pardon of all guilt, pronouncing those who are guilty as "not guilty," and declaring them to be righteous.
Believe fully in Jesus Christ (faith)	Regenerates: He puts his Holy Spirit in their lives, renewing, refreshing, and giving them new birth as children of God. It is the beginning of the process of sanctification.
Start the process of discipleship	Adopts the new believer into His family and gives him/her all the privileges included therein.

Repentance is a radical break with sin and an active turning to God.

Repentance
"We believe that repentance, which is a sincere and thorough change of the mind in regard to sin, involving a sense of personal guilt and a voluntary turning away from sin, is demanded of all who have by act or purpose become sinners against God. The Spirit of God gives to all who will repent the gracious help of penitence of heart and hope of mercy, that they may believe unto pardon and spiritual life" (Article of Faith No. 8, Manual of the Church of the Nazarene 2013-2017).

What Does It Mean To Be Justified?

In this section we will study the benefits of salvation.

Justification is an instantaneous legal act of God by which He declares that our sins are forgiven and Christ's righteousness is ours. We are declared blameless before God.

In his letter to the Romans, the Apostle Paul taught about the benefits received by the person who has been justified:

- **The one who is justified is a blessed person** (4:7-8). The apostle Paul uses the same expression that Jesus used in the Sermon on the Mount (Matthew 5). In the original language this means: How happy is…! In this sense, it is not just a statement but a cry: "Blessed are those whose sin the Lord will never count against them."

- **Justification brings peace** (5:1-5). When Paul talks about peace here it is not just the product of mental discipline or peace that an individual can create for himself or herself, but this peace comes from the assurance of having been forgiven by God.

- **The person who has been justified has hope in the glory of God** (5:2). The person who is saved has confidence in Christ Jesus. He/she is a person looking at the future with hope, having faith in others, trusting that God will fulfill all His promises and will always be the loving Father.

In the illustration below you can see the process of salvation, ranging from the position of human sin, to the position of joy and happiness that arises from the restored relationship with God through Jesus Christ:

Life of joy and hope in God

Regenerated, adopted

Justified, saved, reconciled

Repentant and believers

Sinners and enemies of God

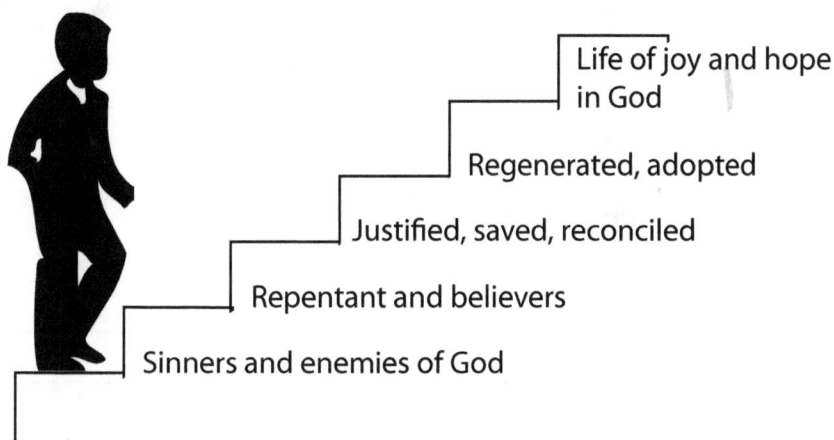

To sin is to disobey and rebel against the known will of God. Sin may include bad thoughts, rejecting God, idolizing oneself, being selfish, trusting one's own human efforts, behaving in a way that God does not like or refusing to obey God's specific instructions. It literally means "missing the mark." For Wesley, "Sin is a willful transgression of a known law" (Orton Wiley: Introduction to Christian Theology, 194).

The Meaning of Forgiveness
Through forgiveness God wipes out, removes, destroys or takes away the obstacles that stand between man and God and between man and his fellow man (Isaiah 38:17, Micah 7:19).

WHAT DID WE LEARN?

All human beings are separated from God because they are guilty before a righteous judge of committing sin. The only way to be rid of personal sin and its consequences has been provided by God in Jesus Christ, who by dying in our place on the cross, made it possible for everyone who believes in Him to be forgiven and to live a new life, enjoying eternal peace and fellowship with God (John 3:16).

Activities

INSTRUCTIONS:

1. Mention some qualities in your life that reflect the image of God.

_____

_____

_____

2. In your own words, explain what a person should do to be free of sin.

_____

_____

_____

_____

_____

3. Read Colossians 2:13-14 and 3:3. Then complete the following sentences:

a) You were _____ in your sins before God saved you.

b) The debt owed for sins has been _____ by Christ and _____ to the Cross.

c) Those that live in Christ have died to _____.

4. What does God do with our sins according to Psalms 103:12, Isaiah 43:25 and Hebrews 10:16-17?

_____

_____

_____

_____

5. Share a brief testimony in a small group about how your life has changed since you have been forgiven of your sins.

HOW CAN I BE SANCTIFIED?

Objectives
- To acknowledge that God's desire is that all live holy lives.
- To value the experience of entire sanctification.
- To desire a continuous progress in the holy life.

Main Ideas
- Sanctification takes place in a Christian's life through the filling of the Holy Spirit.
- Sanctification gives the Christian power to manifest God's love in his/her life by serving others.
- To be filled with the Holy Spirit, one must desire to wholeheartedly live for God, die to self and give up everything which might hinder serving God.

Introduction

Can a Christian be holy? In this part of the lesson we will examine what the Nazarenes affirm concerning sanctification. Article of Faith, Number 10 of the Church of the Nazarene states:

John Wesley summed up the term sanctification as "the manifestation of love."

*"We believe that **sanctification** is that work of God, which transforms believers into the likeness of Christ. It is wrought by God's grace through the Holy Spirit in initial sanctification, or regeneration (simultaneous with justification), entire sanctification, and the continued perfecting work of the Holy Spirit culminating in glorification. In glorification we are fully conformed to the image of the Son.*

We believe that entire sanctification is that act of God, subsequent to regeneration, by which believers are made free from original sin, or depravity, and brought into a state of entire devotement to God, and the holy obedience of love made perfect.

It is wrought by the baptism with or infilling of the Holy Spirit, and comprehends in one experience the cleansing of the heart from sin and the abiding, indwelling presence of the Holy Spirit, empowering the believer for life and service.

Entire sanctification is provided by the blood of Jesus, is wrought instantaneously by grace through faith, preceded by entire consecration; and to this work and state of grace the Holy Spirit bears witness.

This experience is also known by various terms representing its different phases, such as "Christian perfection," "perfect love," "heart purity," "the baptism with or infilling of the Holy Spirit," "the fullness of the blessing," and "Christian holiness."

We believe that there is a marked distinction between a pure heart and a mature character. The former is obtained in an instant, the result of entire sanctification; the latter is the result of growth in grace.

We believe that the grace of entire sanctification includes the divine impulse to grow in grace as a Christlike disciple. However, this impulse must be consciously nurtured and careful attention given to the requisites and processes of spiritual development and improvement in Christlikeness of character and personality. Without such purposeful endeavor, one's witness may be impaired and the grace itself frustrated and ultimately lost. Participating in the means of grace, especially the fellowship, disciplines, and sacraments of the Church, believers grow in grace and in wholehearted love to God and neighbor" (Manual, Church of the Nazarene 2013-2017).

What Is Sanctification?

Entire sanctification is being filled with the love of God.

As Wesleyans, we understand that the process of sanctification begins in the experience of conversion or new birth, where God baptizes us with His Holy Spirit. After this first experience of salvation, the Bible teaches about a second work of grace necessary in the Christian life. This is not optional, but necessary for one to remain strong and grow in this new life and become Christlike.

Nazarenes believe that there comes a time when the new creature in Christ understands that he/she needs to be delivered from the sinful condition inside which fights against their willingness to be obedient in everything to their Lord. The individual is not to be blamed for this condition that has been passed down him by inheritance from Adam and thus to all human beings.

This sinful condition encourages people to seek to satisfy their own selfish desires instead of seeking first God's will. The Christian who lives in this state feels guilty for these tendencies, of which he or she cannot be freed by his or her own strength or will (Psalm 51:7; Acts 15:8-9; Ephesians 5:25-27; 1 John 1:7). Paul describes this condition as the "carnal mind" (Romans 8:6), "the law of sin and death" (Romans 8:2), the "old nature" and the "body of sin" (Romans 6:6), and the "root of bitterness" (Hebrews 12:15).

John Wesley summed up sanctification as "the manifestation of love." Only when we are completely filled with the Holy Spirit can we love God and others with our whole being. Jesus summed up God's will for our life as a life of perfect love: *"Love the Lord your God with all your heart and with all your soul and with all your mind and with all your strength...Love your neighbor as yourself. There is no commandment greater than these"* (Mark 12:30-31).

The Bible teaches that sanctification is:

1. A commandment of God (Matthew 5:48; 22:37, 39).

2. The purpose of God for His children. By his love and mercy, God wants us to share His divine nature (John 17:20-23, Ephesians 3:14, 19; 1 Thessalonians 5:23).

3. Power of God. Through the Holy Spirit, God wants to share with us His power and authority (Acts 1:8).

Original sin is man's first transgression of God's law. The sin of Adam and Eve passed to all humans from generation to generation and so all mankind has inherited Adam's sinful nature.

4. A promise of God. He has promised to make us holy if we are ready to walk according to His will (Deuteronomy 30:6; Psalm 130:8; Ezekiel 36:25,29; Romans 8:3-4; 2 Corinthians 7:1; Ephesians 5:25-27 and 1 John 3:8).

Is This Experience for Everyone?

Holiness is God's will for all His children.

"Therefore, since we have these promises, dear friends, let us purify ourselves from everything that contaminates body and spirit, perfecting holiness out of reverence for God" (2 Corinthians 7:1 NIV).

The New Testament tells us that our sanctification is God's will; in other words, we are to be holy before Him and our neighbor. That is why Jesus prayed to His Father that the disciples and those who would believe in Him in future generations would be sanctified in truth (John 17:19-20).

In 1 Thessalonians 5:23 Paul says, *"May God himself, the God of peace, sanctify you through and through. May your whole spirit, soul and body be kept blameless at the coming of our Lord Jesus Christ."* This verse has five lessons:

1. Sanctification is God's work. Scripture itself declares this. God is holy and wants us to be holy as He is.

2. Sanctification is complete. The apostle desires that the Christian be sanctified completely, that is, in mind, soul and body.

3. Sanctification is for this life. It is not necessary to wait until death to be sanctified. Sanctification is for this life as well as for eternal life.

4. Sanctification reaches every part of human nature. "Your whole spirit, soul and body" means the total being of the person; your emotions, will, thoughts and motivations have to be sanctified.

5. Sanctification prepares Christians for the Lord's coming and for the final judgment. Therefore, entire sanctification should not be postponed until the Lord Jesus Christ returns, but needs to be sought NOW, because the Christian, who cooperates with God in this process of sanctification, will be found blameless when Jesus comes back.

Just as the believers in Thessalonica, all who have accepted Christ as their Lord and Savior need to grow continuously as they are transformed in accordance with the character of Jesus Christ.

The Human Part in Sanctification

How does the believer prepare for the filling of the Spirit?

John Wesley taught that there are three factors that prepare the believer to be entirely sanctified.

Repentance is the first factor. This repentance is different from that which precedes the conversion experience. This does not arise from the guilt of sin committed, but from the discovery of the sinful desires that dwell in the Christian's being, from which he/she cannot escape no matter how hard they try.

The second factor is the desire to die to sin; the desire to be free from every trace of sin that dwells in our being. The third factor is faith: trusting that God will deliver us from this inclination to sin. Faith makes it possible to believe that God will work within to bring this desired purification (Acts 15:8-9, 26:18, Galatians 6:14).

In the experience of entire sanctification, the human being plays an important role. Responding to God's love is a decision that the person must make, devoting his or her entire being completely to the Lord to use as He sees fit.

> The filling of the Spirit is required for any service to God: "…choose seven men from among you who are known to be **full of the Spirit** and wisdom. We will turn this responsibility over to them" (Acts 6:3 NIV).

The act of consecration has its roots in the Old Testament. The people of Israel were asked to consecrate themselves to serve the Lord (Joshua 3:5). In the New Testament, the attitude required of us is "to offer" or "to present" our whole being to God (Romans 6:13, 19, 12:1) and this act of consecration can only be done by a person who has been born again (Romans 6:13).

The apostle Paul taught that every Christian is called to present their entire being as a living sacrifice, pleasing to God (Romans 12:1). This voluntary self-sacrifice or offering comes from a grateful heart in response to God's love.

The Christian consecrates his/herself by prayer. This is a prayer that includes dedicating one's life, abilities and possessions, now, as well as in the future to God; it is a complete surrender to a life of service to God.

The Divine Part in Sanctification

What does God do to purify the heart?

The action of God in sanctification is to fill His children with the Holy Spirit, purifying and cleansing them from sin, and making them holy. This is something that the Christian cannot do.

In entire sanctification the whole being, spirit, soul and body, is subject to the lordship of Christ (Romans 8:7). However, this experience does not make one perfect, in the sense that it is impossible to have wrong thoughts or actions. But in sanctification, the Lord purifies the intentions of the heart so that the Christian's thoughts, speech and actions are continually directed to doing what is pleasing to God.

It is possible for the sanctified person to sin. Christians must take great care of salvation, living in continual obedience, examining the life daily and being obedient to the guidance of the Holy Spirit, who corrects and leads to be more and more like Christ (Philippians 2:12). The decision to live in purity and serve God with all our strength must be renewed every day.

This second work of grace has different names such as the sanctification of the believer, entire consecration, perfection of love or the filling of the Spirit. It is through this experience that the believer, now sanctified, wants to obey the will of God one hundred percent. In sanctification, human nature is truly changed into harmony with the will of God, and the image of God is renewed in his children (1 Thessalonians 5:23).

Entire sanctification is not the final step in the life of the believer, but the beginning of a life of growth "in the grace and knowledge of our Lord and Savior Jesus Christ" (2 Peter 3:18).

"May God himself, the God of peace, sanctify you through and through. May your whole spirit, soul and body be kept blameless at the coming of our Lord Jesus Christ" (1 Thessalonians 5:23 NIV).

Suggestions for further study:

Sanctification	
Jeremiah 31:31-34	1 John 1:7-9
Ezekiel 36:25-27	2 Corinthians 6:14-7:1
Malachi 3:2-3	Galatians 2:20; 5:16-25
Matthew 3:11-12	Ephesians 3:14-21; 5:17-18, 25-27
Luke 3:16-17	Philippians 3:10-15
John 7:37-39; 14:15-23; 17:6-20	Colossians 3:1-17
Acts 1:5; 2:1-4; 15:8-9	1 Thessalonians 5:23-24
Romans 6:11-13; 19; 8:1-4; 12:1-12	Hebrews 4:9-11; 10:10-17; 12:1-2; 13:12

Christian perfection or perfect love	
Deuteronomy 30:6	Philippians 3:10-15
Matthew 5:43-48; 22:37-40	Hebrews 6:1
Romans 12:9-21; 13:8-10	I John 4:17-18
1 Corinthians 13	

Baptism with the Holy Spirit	
Jeremiah 31: 31-34	1 Peter 1:22
Ezekiel 36: 25-27	1 John 3:3
Malachi 3:2-3	Acts 1:5; 2:1-4; 15: 8-9
Matthew 3:11-12	Romans 15:29
Luke 3:16-17	

Christian Holiness	
Matthew 5:1 – 7:29	1 Thessalonians 3:13; 4:7-8; 5:23
John 15:1-11	2 Timothy 2:19-22
Romans 12:1-15:3	Hebrews 10:19-25; 12:14; 13:20-21
2 Corinthians 7:1	1 Peter 1:15-16
Ephesians 4:17-5:20	2 Peter 1:1-11; 3:18
Philippians 1:9-11; 3:12-15	Jude 20 and 21
Colossians 2:20-3:17	

Entire sanctification is an instantaneous work of God, but it also is a process by which the Christian grows to become more like Jesus.

WHAT DID WE LEARN?

Entire sanctification or fullness of the Spirit is God's will for all His children. To receive this second experience subsequent to conversion, believers must surrender their whole lives as an offering to God's service. In response, God purifies the heart of all evil inclination and fills the believer with His Holy Spirit. It is through the filling of the Spirit that God's perfect love develops and grows in the our lives, making us more and more like Christ, enabling us to love as Christ does.

INSTRUCTIONS:

1. Why is it God's will that we should be sanctified?

_____
_____
_____

2. What other names are used for the experience of entire sanctification?

_____
_____
_____

3. Who can receive the experience of entire sanctification and why?

_____
_____
_____

4. In your opinion, what are the obstacles that prevent a child of God from being filled with the Spirit?

     1._____
     2._____
     3._____

5. In pairs, share your views about the following question: If a person asks, "Why do I need to be filled with the Spirit?" what would be your answer?

Then choose two of the best answers from each group and share them with the rest of the class.

_____
_____
_____
_____
_____
_____
_____
_____

WHAT IS THE PURPOSE OF THE CHURCH?

Introduction

What is the Church? Is it just a human organization? How did the Church emerge?

In Article of Faith, number 11, which concerns the Church, the Nazarene Manual states:

"We believe in the Church, the community that confesses Jesus Christ as Lord, the covenant people of God made new in Christ, the Body of Christ called together by the Holy Spirit through the Word. God calls the Church to express its life in the unity and fellowship of the Spirit; in worship through the preaching of the Word, observance of the sacraments, and ministry in His name; by obedience to Christ, holy living, and mutual accountability.

The mission of the Church in the world is to share in the redemptive and reconciling ministry of Christ in the power of the Spirit. The Church fulfills its mission by making disciples through evangelism, education, showing compassion, working for justice, and bearing witness to the kingdom of God. The Church is a historical reality, which organizes itself in culturally conditioned forms; exists both as local congregations and as a universal body; sets apart persons called of God for specific ministries. God calls the Church to live under His rule in anticipation of the consummation at the coming of our Lord Jesus Christ" (Manual of the Church of the Nazarene 2013-2017).

To study more about the church:

Exodus 19:3, Jeremiah 31:33, Matthew 8:11, 10:7, 16:13-19, 24, 18:15-20, 28:19-20, John 17:14-26, 20:21 - 23, Acts 1:7-8, 2:32-47, 6:1-2, 13:1, 14:23, Romans 2:28-29, 4:16, 10:9-15, 11:13 - 32, 12:1-8, 15:1-3, 1 Corinthians 3:5-9, 7:17, 11:1, 17-33, 12:3, 12:31, 14:26-40, 2 Corinthians 5:11-6:1, Galatians 5:6,13-14; 6:1-5,15, Galatians 5:6, 13-14, 6:1-5, 15, Ephesians 4:1-17, 5:25-27, Philippians 2:1-16, 1 Thessalonians 4:1-12, 1 Timothy 4:13, Hebrews 10:19-25, 1 Peter 1:1-2, 13, 2:4-12, 21; 4:1-2, 10-11, 1 John 4:17, Jude 24, Revelation 5:9-10.
(Article of Faith, XI)

How Did the Church Emerge?

In this section we will learn about the beginnings of the Church.

From the beginning of human history, God wanted to form His people. For this purpose, He called Abraham. God promised Abraham that his descendants would be a great nation who would be a blessing to all the families of the Earth (Genesis 12:1-9). Over time, Israel became the nation chosen by the Lord, but the people easily forgot the mission of being a light to the nations that God had entrusted to them. Later, God proclaimed through the prophets that His people would be from all nations and these, His people, are the Church (1 Peter 2:9-10).

In spite of the poor performance of Israel in their mission, God fulfilled His purposes and sent His Son Jesus Christ, who through His ministry, death and resurrection, began the ministry of the Church through His disciples, giving them the responsibility to preach the gospel to every creature (Matthew 28:18-20).

Christians mark the birth of the Church as the day of Pentecost, when the hundred and twenty disciples gathered in the Upper Room; after a long period of prayer, they were filled with the Holy Spirit and began to evangelize and make disciples of people from many nations gathered in the city of Jerusalem (Acts 2:1-42).

Characteristics of the Church

How do we distinguish the true Church of Jesus Christ?

Traditionally, theologians see some special features in the Church of Christ that distinguish it. For example:

1. The Lord's Church is visible and yet invisible. It is visible because we can see our brothers and sisters in local congregations, but it is invisible because it is comprised of Christians of generations that have lived and are now in the Lord's presence.

2. The church is local and the Church is universal. It is local when referring to the group of believers who gather in one place. It is universal, comprising all believers of all races and of all times.

3. The Church is one and diverse. The unity of the Church comes from being one in Christ. But it is diverse because it is manifested in different local congregations.

4. The Church is both holy and imperfect. Since Christ is holy, the spiritual Body of Christ, the Church, is also holy; however, since it is made up of people, the Church continually needs to be cleansed of sin.

Metaphors of the Church

Through biblical metaphors we can learn more about the Church.

When the Bible teaches truths about the Church of Christ, many times comparisons, parables or figures are used. We will explore what some of the metaphors of the Church teach us in the following table:

Is the Church the building or the people?
According to the Bible, church is not the place or building where we gather to worship God. The church is the group of people who gather to worship, to learn from their Lord and fellowship together (2 Corinthians 6:16). Whenever the church gathers, it is because God has called them to join together before sending them into the world to serve Him.

"For just as each of us has one body with many members, and these members do not all have the same function, so in Christ we, though many, form one body, and each member belongs to all the others" (Romans 12:4-5).

Biblical Metaphors of the Church	Biblical Text	Main Teaching
A flock of sheep	John 10:1-18	Jesus is the Good Shepherd who cares, nourishes and defends his church (flock), to the point that He gave his life for His flock.
The bride of Christ	Revelation 19:7-8	Jesus Christ is the bridegroom who comes to wed the Church that is preparing to be holy for the marriage of the Lamb, an event that will occur at the Second Coming.
A building	Ephesians 2:19-22	The foundations of the Church are the apostles and prophets; the cornerstone that holds all the building together is Christ. This building is a holy temple and dwelling place of the Spirit and is continuously growing by adding more disciples.
Body of Christ	Romans 12:3-8; 1 Corinthians 12:12-27	The Church is united to Christ, the spiritual leader (head). Its members help each other and everyone carries out a special job (ministry), exercising the gifts of the Spirit.
People of God (holy nation)	1 Peter 2:9	Just as God chose Israel from among the other nations to be His holy people, so the Church has been chosen to be the new people of God.

Christians are a royal priesthood
As priests, Christians have the privilege to intercede in prayer before God for sinners, so that they may devote their lives to Christ and be saved.

The Body of Christ was one of Paul's favorite descriptions when referring to the Church (1 Corinthians 10:16, 12:27).

The Sacraments or Means of Grace

This section explores the practices mandated by Jesus.

The sacraments are those practices and celebrations that have been ordained by Jesus that the Church carries out. These are very important because they communicate fundamental teachings of the Christian faith, help affirm the identity as the people of God, build community among the brethren, and share the presence of Christ through the Holy Spirit's activity.

The New Bible Dictionary explains the meaning of sacrament as follows: "an outward and visible sign, ordained by Christ, setting forth and pledging an inward and spiritual blessing" (Marshall 1034).

Not all faiths have the same view concerning the meaning of the sacraments. For example, the Roman Catholic Church and the Greek Orthodox Church celebrate seven sacraments: baptism, communion, confirmation, penance, extreme unction, ordination and matrimony. But most Protestant churches acknowledge only two sacraments: baptism and communion, these being the only ones instituted by Jesus Christ (Matthew 28:19, 26:26-27).

The Lord's Supper or Communion

This sacrament is a spiritual feast of communion with Christ.

The Manual for the Church of the Nazarene, in Article of Faith Number 13, states:

"We believe that the Memorial and Communion Supper instituted by our Lord and Savior Jesus Christ is essentially a New Testament sacrament, declarative of His sacrificial death, through the merits of which believers have life and salvation and promise of all spiritual blessings in Christ. It is distinctively for those who are prepared for reverent appreciation of its significance, and by it they show forth the Lord's death till He come again. It being the Communion feast, only those who have faith in Christ and love for the saints should be called to participate therein" (Manual of the Church of the Nazarene, 2013-2017).

In 1 Corinthians 10:14 to 11:26, the Apostle Paul teaches the Church the importance of celebrating the Lord's Supper frequently.

1. Paul contrasts the pagan communion with their idols and the communion of the Christian with Christ.

2. This is a teaching that the Church has received directly from the Lord. From the point of view of Paul, the Lord's Supper replaced the Jewish holiday of Passover. This is because Communion is a feast of remembrance of the means employed for our spiritual liberation, that is, the body and blood of Jesus shed for us on the cross of Calvary. The bread that is shared represents the body of Christ and grape juice represents His blood.

3. It is a festival that commemorates and celebrates in advance the promise of the return of our Lord Jesus Christ for the second time.

4. The Lord´s supper expresses the unity of the members of the Church. In verse 10:17 Paul declares: *"Because there is one loaf, we, who are many, are one body, for we all share the one loaf."*

5. It is a new opportunity to give thanks for the new life that God has given us by His great love and mercy. Each time we participate in this sacrament, to which the Lord calls us, we celebrate and remember that God through His Son Jesus Christ provided our salvation at a high price.

The word sacrament comes from sacrum, meaning sacred.

To study more about the sacraments:
1 Corinthians 10:14-22, 11:23-24
Acts 8:26-39
Romans 6:1-13.

Baptism

This section will explore the significance of baptism.

From Old Testament times, the Jews baptized those who had belonged to other people groups and religions, but wanted to convert to Judaism. John the Baptist, the forerunner of Jesus, baptized in the Jordan River those who repented of their sins and wanted to begin to live in obedience to God (Matthew 3:1-12).

Before ascending to heaven, Jesus told his disciples: *"All authority in heaven and on earth has been given to me. Therefore go and make disciples of all nations, baptizing them in the name of the Father and of the Son and of the Holy Spirit, and teaching them to obey everything I have commanded you. And surely I am with you always, to the very end of the age"* (Matthew 28:18-20).

In his first sermon, Peter preached the following: *"Repent and be baptized, every one of you, in the name of Jesus Christ for the forgiveness of your sins. And you will receive the gift of the Holy Spirit"* (Acts 2:38). Therefore, to participate in the sacrament of baptism, it was necessary to believe in Christ and repent.

William Barclay says that for the early Christians (Acts 8:26-39), baptism meant at least three things:

Three forms of baptism:
- Sprinkling water
- Pouring a little water
- Immersion: immersing the body in water

1. Purification of sin. Water has always been a symbol of cleansing.

2. It marked a defining moment in life. It is the beginning of a new life as a disciple of Jesus.

3. It was a true union with Christ. Being submerged in water is like dying and being buried, like Christ; and like the Master, the Christian also rises to a new life (Romans 6:1-4).

The Church of the Nazarene emphasizes in Article of Faith, number 12, the value of the sacrament of baptism to affirm the new disciple in the Christian life:

To study more about baptism, refer to these Scriptures: Matthew 3:1-7, 28:16-20, Acts 2:37-41, 8:35-39, 10:44-48, 16:29-34, 19:1-6, Romans 6:3-4, Galatians 3:26-28, Colossians 2:12, 1 Peter 3:18-22.

*"We believe that Christian **baptism,** commanded by our Lord, is a sacrament signifying acceptance of the benefits of the atonement of Jesus Christ, to be administered to believers and declarative of their faith in Jesus Christ as their Savior, and full purpose of obedience in holiness and righteousness. **Baptism** being a symbol of the new covenant, young children may be baptized, upon request of parents or guardians who shall give assurance for them of necessary Christian training. Baptism may be administered by sprinkling, pouring, or immersion, according to the choice of the applicant"(Manual, Church of the Nazarene 2013-2017, bold text added).*

Five Main Functions of the Church

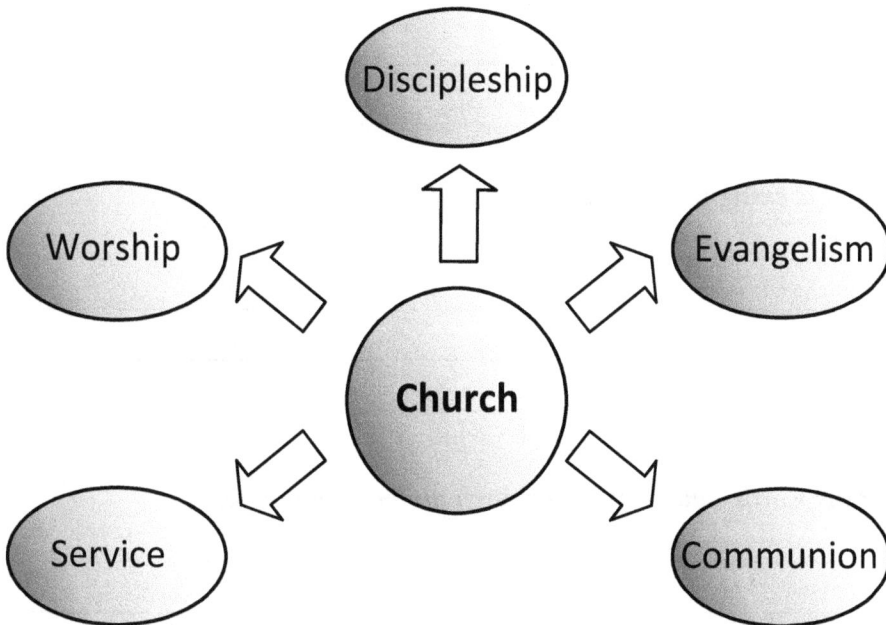

To study more about the Lord's Supper, refer to these Scriptures:
Exodus 12:1-14, Matthew 26:26-29, Mark 14:22-25, Luke 22:17-20, John 6:28-58, 1 Corinthians 10:14-21, 11:23-32.

A certain missionary who used to baptize his converts in a river, asked them to enter by one bank of the river and after baptizing them, he encouraged them to leave by the other bank to indicate that baptism had drawn a line that sent them in a new direction in life.

WHAT DID WE LEARN?

Jesus Christ founded the Church so that His disciples would gather together to worship, feed on the Word, fellowship, and through their service to the world through evangelism, make disciples for Christ. The Church is holy and divine in nature, but also human and imperfect. Jesus established two sacraments: baptism as a symbol of the new birth as a disciple, and communion, a permanent reminder of the union of His people to their Lord.

1. What is the origin and purpose of the existence of the church?

_____
_____
_____
_____

2. Can you explain the reason that the words sanctuary and church are not synonymous?

_____
_____
_____
_____

3. Complete the following acrostic on the Church according to the material studied in this lesson.

A. C _ _ _ _ _ _ _ _
B. _ H _ _ _
C. _ _ _ U _
D. _ _ _ _ _ R _ _ _
E. C _ _ _ _ _ _ _
F. _ _ _ _ H _ _

A. Another name of the sacrament of the Lord's Supper.

B. One of the Pauline metaphors of the Church.

C. Founder of the Church

D. The Church made up of all believers of all races and ages.

E. Baptism is the sign of the new _____.

F. One of the functions of the Church.

WHAT DOES THE BIBLE SAY ABOUT THE FUTURE?

Objectives

- To clarify the meaning of "Kingdom of Heaven."
- To identify the events of the Second Coming of Christ.
- To learn about the final judgment and eternal life.

Main Ideas

-The Kingdom of God is a past reality, a present reality and a future reality.
-There are several events in the history of salvation that are yet to come, such as the final judgment, the punishment of God's enemies and the reward for His faithful people.
-The Kingdom of righteousness of Jesus Christ will be fully established in His Second Coming.

Introduction

It is normal to feel curious about the second coming of Christ, but we must accept that there are things that God has kept for himself, because He only needs to know them (Acts 1:7). What we do know is that Jesus Christ can come at any time; therefore, we must always be prepared, living in holiness.

There are different interpretations concerning the events of the Second Coming. The majority of them lack a serious Scriptural basis. Many people preach, write books and even make movies on how and when the "great tribulation," the rapture of the Church, and the revelation of the antichrist will take place, and in doing so they create confusion about how these events will unfold.

It is important to remember that since Jesus ascended to heaven there have been those who claim to know the day and the hour of His coming, but we must not be misled since Jesus himself said that the only one who knows the day or hour of His coming is the Heavenly Father (Matthew 24:36).

In this lesson we will only study what the Church of the Nazarene, based on the Bible, believes and teaches about future events surrounding the coming of the eternal Kingdom of Jesus Christ.

The Kingdom of God

Where does it come from? Where and when will the Kingdom of God happen?

The theme of the Kingdom of God is very important to understanding both present and future events. For this reason, it is essential to understand what the Scriptures are referring to when they speak about the Kingdom of God.

The Lord Jesus Christ was the one who taught most clearly about the Kingdom. He proclaimed that His message was "the gospel of the kingdom" (Matthew 4:12, 13:17). Jesus taught that the Kingdom of God came into the world with Him and that His authority as King of this Kingdom is unlimited.

The theme of the Kingdom of God is one of the most discussed topics of Christian theology because there are so many different interpretations. One of the most widespread in our context is what the Roman Catholic Church once believed, which states that everything that does not belong to the Roman Catholic Church is outside the Kingdom of God. This interpretation limits the Kingdom of God to a human organization, and it is the same assumption that sectarian groups such as the Jehovah's Witnesses and Mormons make.

However, when we study the Bible we can see clearly that this Kingdom is not limited to an organization, but extends to all the children of God. This Kingdom is divided into three historic times since it has had its beginning, is spreading today and will exist forever.

1.) The Kingdom came with Christ, who is the King. This Kingdom, like any other, has its own laws, but in this case, the laws are written in the hearts of those who belong to Him.

2) The Kingdom is expanding, gaining territory with each new life that accepts Christ as Savior and Lord.

3) The Kingdom will come to its fullness at the Second Coming of Christ, when his boundless and eternal rule over his people and all creation will be established (Mark 1:14-15).

In conclusion, the Kingdom of God is present in this world right now in the life of each person living under the Lordship of Jesus Christ (Matthew 12:22-28; 13:44-46, Mark 4:3; 12:34, Luke 17:20-21).

The Second Coming of Christ

What do Nazarenes believe about the Second Coming of Christ?

When Jesus came the first time, he had a mission to accomplish in preaching the good news of the Kingdom of God, and consummating the plan of salvation by being crucified, dying and coming back to life again (Acts 10:39-41). Part of His mission was to establish His Church so that His work could continue through His believers; He commissioned the Church to make disciples for the Kingdom in all nations (Acts 10:42-43).

Jesus promised His Church that He would come again in all power and glory (Acts 1:11). In the New Testament this event is described by the Greek word parousia which means being present or presence (2 Corinthians 4:1-3). This word is also translated as a coming or arrival (1 Thessalonians 4:13).

The Church of the Nazarene does not speculate on the order of future events or on the day when Jesus will come again. In Article of Faith number 15 on the "Second Coming of Christ," the Manual states:

"We believe that the Lord Jesus Christ will come again; that we who are alive at His coming shall not precede them that are asleep in Christ Jesus; but that, if we are abiding in Him, we shall be caught up with the risen saints to meet the

The meaning of the word "kingdom," basileia in the Greek, has two meanings: one meaning refers to concrete "domains," "territory," "kingdoms" or "people governed by the king;" the second one is more abstract indicating "sovereignty" or "royal power." When you say you preach "the gospel of the Kingdom of God," this kingdom does not refer to a geographical point, but to the sovereignty of God.

As for the time of its fulfillment, the prophecies of the Bible have been classified into three types:

1. Prophecies already fulfilled. These refer to the people of Israel and Judah, to the first coming of Jesus Christ and the establishment of the Church through the coming of the Holy Spirit who lives in the hearts of the sons and daughters of God.

2. Prophecies that are in a process of being fulfilled. These are events related to the history of the nation of Israel and the Church.

3. Prophecies not yet fulfilled. These are about the future of Israel and the Church and are especially related to the Second Coming of Jesus Christ and the establishment of God's eternal Kingdom.

Lord in the air, so that we shall ever be with the Lord" (Church of the Nazarene Manual 2013-2017).

Later in Article of Faith, number 16 entitled "Resurrection, Judgment and Destiny" it states:

> *"We believe in the resurrection of the dead, that the bodies both of the just and of the unjust shall be raised to life and united with their spirits—' they that have done good, unto the resurrection of life; and they that have done evil, unto the resurrection of damnation.`*
>
> *We believe in future judgment in which every person shall appear before God to be judged according to his or her deeds in this life.*
>
> *We believe that glorious and everlasting life is assured to all who savingly believe in, and obediently follow, Jesus Christ our Lord; and that the finally impenitent shall suffer eternally in hell"* (Church of the Nazarene Manual 2013-2017).

Therefore, the Church of the Nazarene understands that the Bible presents the history of mankind and the universe in a linear fashion (not a cyclical one) that is progressing according to the plan of God for the time when Jesus Christ will return and God will establish forever his kingdom of eternal justice. The Word teaches that at the time of Christ's return, certain events will occur. These will be discussed briefly in the following sections.

The Resurrection of the Dead

What happens to the spirit when a person dies?

The transition from this life to eternal life is something all human beings experience sooner or later. All will have to go through the experience of death, but this is not the end to human existence, but instead a shift to a different form of existence.

After death, people are still in a state of consciousness, namely, they are still awake, can communicate and feel. Jesus taught that all his children upon death are immediately taken to a place where they stay with him. This place is described as "paradise" (Luke 23:43). Paul describes this experience as pleasant and desirable, for in it the believer is free from the suffering associated with living in the flesh, such as pain, sickness, persecution, and sadness among others (Philippians 1:21-24). But Jesus also described the experience for those who have rejected God as one of continuing pain and suffering (Luke 16: 19-31).

But that's not all because when Christ comes again, all the dead will be resurrected. John 5:28-29 states: *"Do not be amazed at this, for a time is coming when all who are in their graves will hear his voice and come out—those who have done what is good will rise to live, and those who have done what is evil will rise to be condemned."*

The nature of the kingdom is heavenly because it comes from God (Matthew 6:9, 10, 33, 12:28, 21:31 ,43).

The Apostle Paul taught about the Christians' future hope in this kingdom which will come in its fullness with Christ in his Second Coming and will bring perfect righteousness, peace and joy on earth forever (Romans 14:17, Colossians 1:13, 1 Corinthians 6:9, 15:50, Galatians 5:21, Ephesians 5:5, 2 Timothy 4:1,18).

School of Leadership - Principles of the Christian Life

When a person dies, the physical body is converted back to Earth, which is the material from which he or she was created (Genesis 3:19), but the spirit never dies. In the resurrection, the spirit is brought back to life in a new body, which has been transformed and has a different nature (1 Corinthians 15:23, 42-44). It is in this state that each person continues their existence. All human beings will be resurrected (Revelation 20:12,13). Believers will be raised to life, and unbelievers will be resurrected to condemnation (Daniel 12:2; John 5:29).

Those who are alive at the time of the coming of Christ will undergo a transformation like those who have risen, receiving a body for eternity. The Apostle Paul and also John in the book of Revelation add to this event another event where the Lord will meet with His Church forever (1 Thessalonians 4:16-18).

The Second Coming of Christ and the promise of salvation is not only for the sons and daughters of God, but for all of creation that suffers under the pollution of sin (Romans 8:18-21). This doctrine of the Second Coming has been one of the pillars of the Christian faith and the hope that has sustained the Church in every age in the midst of suffering and persecution.

The Final Judgment

What is the final judgment?

Jesus Christ will come as judge to judge all mankind and this will occur after all the dead are resurrected (John 5:22-23, Acts 17:31, 2 Corinthians 5:10). The purpose of this judgment is to punish those who willingly refused to live in obedience to the Word of God and to reward those who were faithful disciples of Jesus Christ.

In this court, every person will be judged according to their deeds, their thoughts, their words and their motivations in this life (Daniel 7:9-10; Ecclesiastes 12:14; Romans 2:16; Jude 14, 15; Revelation 20:11-13). Although cleansing of sin is received by faith and not by works, in the final judgment every good work will be rewarded (2 Corinthians 5:10).

Eternal Life

In this section we will learn about "the heavens."

When Christians speak of "heaven" they actually are referring to eternal life, which is prepared for all the children of God. In other passages of the Bible, this place is referred to as the "holy city," the "new Jerusalem," and "the tabernacle of God" (Revelation 21:2,3).

Although there is little information in the Word about this place, the following has been revealed:

-It is a life of complete happiness, where the believer will be continually in the presence of God (Psalm 16:11) and in perfect communion with God and the Lamb (Revelation 22:3-5).

-It is a place where the glory of Jesus Christ will be revealed in its fullness (John 17:24).

The day of his Second Coming has different names such as: "the Lord's Day," "the coming of the Son of Man" (Matthew 24:27), "the coming of the Lord" (1 Thessalonians 4:15, James 5:7.8), "the coming of the day of God" (2 Peter 3:12) and is described as the beginning of a time of judgment for humanity and of reward for his faithful disciples (Isaiah 2:2-4; 24:21, Daniel 2:44, 7:13-14, Psalm 24, Amos 5:18, Zechariah 8:3, Matthew 26:64, Mark 14:62, Luke 22:69, Acts 1:9-11).

To study more about the Second Coming of Christ, refer to these Scriptures:
Matthew 25:31-46, John 14:1-3, Acts 1:9-11, Philippians 3:20-21, 1 Thessalonians 4:13-18, Titus 2:11-14, Hebrews 9:26-28 2 Peter 3:3-15, Revelation 1:7-8, 22:7-20.

-There, the believer will continue to grow to be like Jesus Christ because he will know Him as He is (I John 3:1-2).

-It is a place of complete holiness. There is no sin, injustice or evil (Isaiah 35:10, Revelation 21:27).

-All creation will give praise, honor and glory to Jesus Christ forever (Revelation 5:13).

Jesus left his disciples, saying he was going to prepare this special place so He could be with His disciples forever (John 14:2-3).

Hell

Is hell a myth or does it really exist?

The Bible teaches that the decisions that human beings make in this life have eternal consequences. Although the common belief is that people can settle accounts with God after death, the Word teaches that nothing that has been done in this life can be changed after death.

Eternity is something that every person will experience, whether they are Christians who have been saved by Christ, Muslims, Buddhists, atheists, or any other belief. The truth is that no human being has control or can change what awaits him after death.

God has revealed that all those who willfully reject the saving grace of the Lord are condemned to an eternal life of suffering in a place called "hell" (Matthew 23:33, Mark 16:16, John 3:17-19).

Like "heaven," hell is a real and concrete place. The word Jesus used to describe this place where God will throw his enemies is *"gehena."* The book of Revelation describes this place as a lake of fire and brimstone (Revelation 21:8).

Contrary to the jokes often made about hell, which describe Satan as the king of this place delightedly tormenting humans, the Bible says that this place is reserved especially for Satan and his demons: *"And the devil, who deceived them, was thrown into the lake of burning sulfur, where the beast and the false prophet had been thrown. They will be tormented day and night for ever and ever"* (Revelation 20:10).

It is not God's will that humans have this ending, but they themselves are condemned when they reject the offer of salvation through Jesus Christ. The only way to escape this fate of sorrow and death is to accept Christ as Savior in order to be registered in the Book of Life:

"Then I saw a great white throne and him who was seated on it. The earth and the heavens fled from his presence, and there was no place for them. And I saw the dead, great and small, standing before the throne, and books were

For further study of future events, refer to these Scriptures:
Genesis 18:25, 1 Samuel 2:10, Psalm 50:6, Isaiah 26:19, Daniel 12:2-3, Matthew 25:31-46, Mark 9:43-48, Luke 16:19-31; 20:27-38, John 3:16 - 18, 5:25-29, 11:21-27, Acts 17:30-31, Romans 2:1-16, 14:7-12, 1 Corinthians 15:12 -58, 2 Corinthians 5:10, 2 Thessalonians 1:5-10, Revelation 20:11-15, 22:1-15, Matthew 22:37-39, 27:34, Romans 12:1-2, 1 Corinthians 6:19-20, 9:24-27.

opened. *Another book was opened, which is the book of life. The dead were judged according to what they had done as recorded in the books. The sea gave up the dead that were in it, and death and Hades gave up the dead that were in them, and each person was judged according to what they had done. Then death and Hades were thrown into the lake of fire. The lake of fire is the second death. Anyone whose name was not found written in the book of life was thrown into the lake of fire"* (Revelation 20:11-15).

The saving grace of the Lord has been provided for everyone, and no one, absolutely no one, needs to be lost in hell; this is the message of hope that every human being needs to hear.

"Therefore keep watch, because you do not know the day or the hour" (Matthew 25:13, NIV).

WHAT DID WE LEARN?

The Church of the Nazarene believes that the Bible teaches that Jesus will come again to judge the living and the dead. At His coming all the dead will be raised with a transformed body. God will reward his faithful children, taking them to a place of eternal life in His presence, a place called heaven. Those who refuse the Lord will be thrown into a place of eternal suffering with the devil and his demons, a place called hell.

Activities

Time  20'

1. In your own words, explain who currently belongs to the Kingdom of God, and who are the enemies of the Kingdom?

_____

_____

_____

_____

2. There is evidence that the Second Coming of Christ may happen at any time … What if it happened this week? Make a list of the things you need to do in your own life this week to be prepared for the Second Coming of Christ.

_____

_____

_____

_____

3. Make a list of the things you need to do to help your family and your church family be ready for the Second Coming of the Lord.

_____

_____

_____

_____

4. Write here the names of people who are close to you who you believe would go to hell if they were to die. Then take time to pray in class, fast one day and pray this week that God will use your life for these people to be saved.

_____

_____

_____

_____

_____

_____

_____

Final evaluation

Time 15'

COURSE: PRINCIPLES OF THE CHRISTIAN LIFE

Name of Student: _____

Church or Study Center: _____

District: _____

Professor: _____

Date of this evaluation: _____

1. Explain in your own words how this course has helped you to appreciate the doctrine of the Church of the Nazarene.

_____

_____

_____

_____

2. Mention a course topic that was beneficial for growth in your Christian life.

_____

_____

_____

_____

3. Do you now have some answers to questions that you had? Describe how this course helped to answer them.

_____

_____

_____

_____

4. What did you learn in the course about ministerial practice?

_____

_____

_____

5. In your opinion, how could this course be improved?

_____

_____

_____

_____

Bibliography

Clarke, Adam. *Comentario de la Santa Biblia III*. Kansas City, Casa Nazarena de Publicaciones: 1974.

Dunning, H. Ray. *Grace, Faith and Holiness*. Kansas City, Beacon Hill Press: 1988.

Grudem, W. *Teología Sistemática* (Tomo I) Miami, Florida, Vida: 2007.

Iglesia del Nazareno. Manual de la Iglesia de Nazareno 2005-2009.

Leonard, Gay. *Artículos de Fe. En que creen los Nazarenos y porqué*. Kansas City, Casa Nazarena de Publicaciones: 2009.

Marshall, I. Howard, Millard, A.R., Packer J.I. and D.J. Wiseman. *New Bible Dictionary*. 3rd edition, Intervarsity Press: 1996.

Mastronardi, Mónica. *Lo que creemos los nazarenos*. San José, C.R. Iglesia del Nazareno, Región MAC: 2002.

Purkiser, W.T. *Explorando Nuestra fe Cristiana*. Kansas City, Casa Nazarena de publicaciones: 1988.

_____ *Creencias para la Vida*. Kansas City, Casa Nazarena de Publicaciones: 1964.

Purkiser, W.T, W.T. R. Taylor, W. Taylor. *Dios, hombre y salvación*. Kansas City, Casa Nazarena de Publicaciones: 1991

Riofrío, Víctor. *Teología Sistemática I. (Módulo del estudiante)*. San José, C.R. Asociación CN-MAC: 2003.

_____ *Teología Sistemática II. (Módulo del profesor)*. San José, C.R. Asociación CN-MAC: 2003.

Taylor, Richard S., Willard H. Taylor y J. Kenneth Grider. *Diccionario Teológico Beacon*. Kansas City, Casa Nazarena de Publicaciones: 1995.

Vine W.E. *Diccionario expositivo de palabras del Antiguo y Nuevo Testamento exhaustivo de Vine*. Nashville, Tennessee, Caribe: 1999.

Wiley Orton. *Introducción a la teología cristiana*. Kansas City, Beacon Hill Press: 1976.

www.ingramcontent.com/pod-product-compliance
Lightning Source LLC
Chambersburg PA
CBHW081222020426

42331CB00012B/3071